Student Course Guide
for

The Writer's Odyssey

Third Edition

Diane Martin, Ph.D.
Professor of English
Dallas County Community College District

TeleLearning

Dallas TeleLearning
R. Jan LeCroy Center for Educational Telecommunications
Dallas County Community College District

For use with *Inventing Arguments*, 3rd edition by John Mauk and John Metz.

WADSWORTH
CENGAGE Learning

Australia • Brazil • Japan • Korea • Mexico • Singapore • Spain • United Kingdom • United States

WADSWORTH
CENGAGE Learning

Requests for permission to make copies of any part of the work should be mailed to:

Dallas TeleLearning
9596 Walnut Street
Dallas, Texas 75243

http://telelearning.dcccd.edu
1-866-347-8576

ISBN: 978-1-133-43407-8
ISBN: 1-133-43407-X

Wadsworth Cengage Learning
20 Channel Center Street
Boston, MA 02210
USA

Cengage Learning is a leading provider of customized learning solutions with office locations around the globe, including Singapore, the United Kingdom, Australia, Mexico, Brazil, and Japan. Locate your local office at:
www.cengage.com/global

Cengage Learning products are represented in Canada by Nelson Education, Ltd.

To learn more about Wadsworth, visit www.cengage.com/wadsworth

Purchase any of our products at your local college store or at our preferred online store www.CengageBrain.com

For product information and technology assistance, contact us at Cengage Learning Customer & Sales Support, 1-800-354-9706

For permission to use material from this text or product, submit all requests online at www.cengage.com/permissions. Further permissions questions can be emailed to permissionrequest@cengage.com

Printed in the United States of America
1 2 3 4 5 6 7 15 14 13 12 11

Printed in the United States of America
1 2 3 4 5   16 15 14 13 12

FD005

Contents

To the Student

Welcome to *The Writer's Odyssey!* You are about to embark upon a writing adventure. You may have enrolled in the previous course to this one, *The Writer's Circle*. Whether you are a lover of writing or not, this course will provide you with the necessary skills, motivation, and tools to understand the writing process and succeed in the college classroom. I encourage you to take advantage of all the tools provided in this engaging experience.

The text, *Inventing Arguments* by John Mauk and John Metz, provides the backdrop and instructional information to complete the requirements in argument and research. When the development team began work, we talked with the authors to discover their philosophy of the writing process and to understand their approach to teaching composition. What you see here is the result of collaboration. I wish to extend my personal thank you to both John Mauk and John Metz for consulting with me as we went through the process of developing this distance learning course.

The video series, *The Writer's Odyssey*, provides you the opportunity to learn more about the writing content and to experience distance-learning students working in collaboration to prepare their argument and research assignments. The program hosts, or "gurus," engage you in a light-hearted manner as they provide instructional content. The diverse students in our writer's group learn from each other as they exchange ideas, suggestions, and feedback about their argument and research assignments and their writing. Sometimes the students struggle with organization, or beginnings and endings; sometimes they find a clear writer's voice. Always the students in the videos are involved in their own writing process. I challenge you to become involved in your own writing. I challenge you to collaborate with others, whether it be your classmates, your spouse, your friends, or your children.

Pay particular attention in the videos to the professional writers who address specific nuances of each lesson. What is counterargument? How do I express an appeal to logic or value? What is MLA documentation? What is APA documentation? How do I locate primary and secondary sources? What is hidden argument? The writers come from many different areas of the writing world: news editors, essayists, novelists, non-fiction writers, lawyers. Their experiences and expertise will encourage your writing. Also included in the videos are "Quick Tips"—short, animated suggestions about very specific topics that can improve your writing, for example, how to use the *Oxford English Dictionary*.

This *Student Course Guide for The Writer's Odyssey* provides you with guidelines for each lesson. Each chapter outlines the lesson goal and objectives, assignments from the text (including an argument handbook and a research guide), and enrichment activities that will assist you in delving deeper into the subject of writing.

Remember the old saying, "Patience is a virtue." As you extend your patience, the text, the videos, the interactive activities, and the student course guide all encourage you to dig deeper, think precisely, and pursue the wonders of the English language. They provide you with outstanding argument and research tools that you will use far into the future after you leave the college atmosphere. I have been an online and classroom instructor for over thirty-five years. Developing this course has been a capstone experience in my career. The gifts of my years of teaching are evident in the results. Please apply your capabilities as you explore the process and joy of writing. Broaden your horizons. Extend your thinking. Argue with objectivity and conviction. Write…revise…and rewrite until you achieve your goal.

—Diane Martin

Course Organization

The Writer's Odyssey is designed as a comprehensive learning package consisting of four elements: student course guide, textbook, video programs, and interactive activities.

STUDENT COURSE GUIDE

The Student Course Guide for this course:

Martin, Diane. *Student Course Guide for The Writer's Odyssey*. 3rd ed. Boston, MA: Cengage Wadsworth, 2013. ISBN (13): 978-1-133-43407-8; ISBN (10): 1-133-43407-X

This student course guide acts as your daily instructor. Each lesson gives you lesson resources, lesson goals, learning objectives, lesson focus points, suggested writing assignments, and enrichment activities. If you follow the student course guide recommendations, read the text assignment, and view each lesson carefully, you should successfully accomplish all of the requirements for this course.

TEXTBOOK

In addition to the student course guide, the textbook for this course is:

Mauk, John and John Metz. *Inventing Arguments*. 3rd ed. Boston, MA: Cengage Wadsworth, 2013. ISBN (13): 978-0-8400-2775-7; (10): 0-8400-2775-3

VIDEO PROGRAMS

The video program series for this course is:

The Writer's Odyssey

Each video program is correlated to a specific reading assignment for that lesson. The video programs are packed with information, so watch them closely.

If the lessons are broadcast more than once in your area, or if DVDs are available at your college, you might find it helpful to watch the video programs again for review. Since essay questions may be taken from the video programs as well as from the textbook, careful attention to both is vital to your success.

COMPUTER-BASED INTERACTIVE ACTIVITIES

Computer-graded interactive exercises and activities are available to students whose institutions have opted to offer these. These activities are useful for reinforcement and review of lesson content and learning objectives. The interactive activities are offered in two formats: DVD-ROM and Internet. Ask your instructor how to access these activities if they are listed in your syllabus as a course requirement.

Course Guidelines

Follow these guidelines as you study the material presented in each lesson:

1. THEME—
   Read the Theme for an introduction to the lesson material.

2. LESSON RESOURCES—
   Review the Lesson Resources in order to schedule your time appropriately. Pay careful attention—the titles and numbers of the textbook chapters, the student course guide lessons, and the video programs may be different from one another.

3. LESSON GOAL—
   Review the Lesson Goal to learn what you are expected to know or be able to do upon completion of the lesson.

4. LESSON LEARNING OBJECTIVES—
   Review the Learning Objectives to guide you in successfully mastering the lesson content and achieving the Lesson Goal.

5. LESSON FOCUS POINTS—
   Pay attention to the Lesson Focus Points to get the most from your reading and viewing. You may want to write responses or notes to reinforce what you learn as you progress through the lesson material.

6. WRITERS INTERVIEWED—
   In Writers Interviewed, we gratefully acknowledge the expertise and assistance offered in the production of *The Writer's Odyssey* video programs by the individuals and institutions listed.

7. SUGGESTED WRITING ASSIGNMENTS—
   The Suggested Writing Assignments are offered as suggestions to help you apply the material presented in the lesson. Consult with your instructor and your course syllabus about the requirements for any of the assignments listed.

8. ENRICHMENT ACTIVITIES—
   The Enrichment Activities will help you evaluate your understanding of the material in this lesson. Use the Answer Key located at the end of the lesson to check your answers or reference material related to each question.

9. ANSWER KEY—
   The Answer Key provides answers and references for the Enrichment Activity questions.

Introduction to Lesson Videos

The video lessons of *The Writer's Odyssey* consist of two distinct but complementary elements: instructional segments that explain concepts and discuss writing tools and strategies, and narrative segments that model the writing process and focus attention on key aspects of the lesson. As you delve into the *The Writer's Odyssey*, you will find that different segments help you accomplish lesson objectives in different ways.

Instructional segments are lively sessions hosted by two writing "gurus," who explain and illustrate the main lesson components. Their teaching points are amplified by commentary from a variety of professional writers, who share their experience and wisdom on the topic at hand. Most lessons are also punctuated with "Quick Tips," animated shorts focusing on specific writing pointers and common pitfalls. This combination of targeted short subjects, interviews with writers, and direct instruction from the gurus serves to introduce new material and deepen your understanding of the skills and strategies of good writing.

Interlaced with the instruction is an ongoing narrative storyline, in which a diverse group of students forms a writer's circle for their mutual support while taking an online composition course focusing on research and argument. They meet regularly in a neighborhood café to discuss assignments and share their work. In each program, you will follow one or more of the students as they undertake the actual writing assignment for that lesson: investigating a topic, refining a thesis, drafting the argument, getting feedback, and rewriting. As their stories unfold, you gain insight into the challenges, frustrations and rewards of producing a thoughtful, provocative piece of writing.

The main characters of *The Writer's Odyssey* represent a broad range of social, racial and ethnic backgrounds. Individually they represent the wide variety of students who can benefit from improving their writing and argument skills, while as a group they model the invaluable support a writer's group can give throughout the writing process. The writer's circle includes:

- **Jada**: African-American, late twenties, Army Reserve. Served in combat in Iraq and is now going to college on the GI bill. Writes a personal blog called JadaSaysSo.
- **Rosa:** Latina, mid-forties, paralegal. Married, children grown or in college. Completing her college degree so she can pursue her life-long dream of going to law school.
- **Marcus:** Asian-American, early twenties, university student. Taking an on-line writing class on top of a full academic load. Majoring in film and working for a film marketing company.
- **Mitch:** Anglo, early twenties, full-time college student, majoring in biology. Passionate about frogs, the environment, ultimate Frisbee, and his way-smart girlfriend.
- **Angie:** Not officially a **member** of the writer's group, but often sits in and gives feedback. A brilliant student and editor of the college paper, she earns her nickname "Encyclopedia Angie."

Lesson 1

Everyday Research

Research is formalized curiosity. It is poking and prying with a purpose.

—Zora Neale Hurston

THEME

Welcome to *The Writer's Odyssey,* a course focused on research and argument. For this first lesson, you will research a personal decision by applying research techniques at home, work, and school.

Making a decision is easier if you set up a plan in advance. Select your criteria first, next do the research, and then you are ready to make a reasoned decision about a life change, attendance at a university, or a product you're thinking of purchasing.

Identifying specific criteria also helps you in the decision-making process. If you were planning to purchase a riding lawnmower, for example, you might consider cost, durability, and usefulness as your governing criteria. Then you would research costs of the various brands of riding lawnmowers, check out the various manufacturers' information for durability, and finally, interview owners who have purchased particular brands of riding lawnmowers.

As you write your essay for this lesson, think carefully about the criteria you will apply to making a personal decision. Criteria are the keys to the process of research and decision-making and must be relevant to the particular subject at hand. Selecting the best and narrowest criteria will make the research phase of your paper more manageable and more interesting for you, the writer. Enjoy your journey!

Research: Finding out what you are going to do when you cannot keep on doing what you are doing now.

—Charles Kettering

LESSON RESOURCES

Textbook: Mauk and Metz: *Inventing Arguments*
- "Note to Students," pp. xxviii–xxx
- Chapter 1, "Inventing Argument," pp. 3–15
- Chapter 2, "Claims," pp. 16–29
- Chapter 3, "Support," pp. 30–63
- Chapter 4, "Opposition," pp. 64–75

Video: "Everyday Research" from the series *The Writer's Odyssey*

LESSON GOAL

You will communicate the ability to apply research and argument to make choices in everyday life.

LESSON LEARNING OBJECTIVES

1. Research information from a variety of sources in order to develop and apply criteria to a decision about an item of personal importance.

2. Incorporate narration, observation, and analysis in writing about the process of using pre-determined criteria to evaluate alternatives in making a personal choice.

3. Use a revision strategy such as peer review to re-examine some aspect of the writing assignment.

4. Examine the theoretical framework of rhetoric and argument.

LESSON FOCUS POINTS

1. What is rhetoric? What is argument?

2. What is the theoretical framework for rhetoric and argument? Why should I understand it for this course?

3. What is rhetorical situation?

4. What are claims? What are the types of claims? What are the characteristics of claims?

Lesson 1—Everyday Research

2

5. What is evidence? List four types of evidence.

6. What are examples? List four types of examples.

7. What are appeals? What is counterargument? What is concession? What are qualifiers?

8. How does a writer develop and apply criteria in making a personal decision?

9. What is narration? How is narrative useful to writers?

10. What is observation? How is observation useful in writing?

11. What is analysis? How is analysis useful?

12. Why is the use of detail important to the writing of an essay?

13. What is voice? How does the writer reveal voice?

14. What should the writer include in an essay about personal research?

15. How is peer revision helpful in the revision of essays?

WRITERS INTERVIEWED

Andy Alford, Assistant Metro Editor, *Austin American Statesman,* Austin, TX

Elizabeth Crook, Author and Novelist, Austin, TX

Ben Fong-Torres, Journalist, San Francisco, CA

Adam Pitluk, Author and Novelist, Dallas, TX

James Ragland, Columnist, *The Dallas Morning News,* Dallas, TX

Robert Rivard, Editor, *San Antonio Express News,* San Antonio, TX

Bob Ray Sanders, Editorial Columnist, *Fort Worth Star-Telegram,* Fort Worth, TX

Hampton Sides, Author, Santa Fe, NM

Gretchen Sween, Attorney and Writer, Susman Godfrey, LLP, Dallas, TX

Mike Trimble, Editor and Columnist, *Denton Record-Chronicle,* Denton, TX

Judy Yung, Historian and Author, Santa Cruz, CA

SUGGESTED WRITING ASSIGNMENTS

Consult with your instructor and the course syllabus about requirements for any of the assignments listed below.

1. Write an essay that includes narration, observation, and analysis of the process undertaken to make an argument for an item of personal importance.

2. Write an observation about your career choice. Discuss how a college education teaches individuals in your field to view the world in a particular way.

> *The practical man is the adventurer, the investigator, the believer in research, the asker of questions, the man who refuses to believe that perfection has been attained. There is no thrill or joy in merely doing that which any one can do. It is always safe to assume, not that the old way is wrong, but that there may be a better way.*
>
> —Henry R. Harrower

ENRICHMENT ACTIVITIES

Complete the following activities. An answer key and/or guidelines appear at the end of this lesson for each activity.

I. Writing Activity: Invention
    Invention assists you in beginning your journey through the development of an essay. For this exercise, select a topic, determine criteria, and then explore the topic. Fill in the following blanks as you develop your topic. If required, submit your responses to your instructor for evaluation.

1. Select a topic. (Find a point of tension.)

    _____

    _____

    _____

    _____

    _____

    _____

    _____

Lesson 1—Everyday Research

4

2. List at least three criteria for your topic. (Be sure they are specific and relevant.)

_____

_____

_____

_____

_____

_____

_____

3. Develop a thesis. (Commit to your own stance and craft a position.)

_____

_____

_____

_____

_____

_____

_____

4. Develop support. (List possible strategies to arrange and communicate your ideas using narration, observation, and analysis.)

_____

_____

_____

_____

_____

II. Writing Activity: Chapter 1: Reading Argument

Your review of Chapter 1 in the textbook will contribute greatly to your success in this course. Use the chapter to review the following terms and definitions.

TERMS AND DEFINITIONS

A. *Five canons of rhetoric*: invention, delivery, arrangement, style or voice, memory

B. *Allusion*: a reference to some public knowledge from history, current events, popular culture, religion, or literature

C. *Narration*: storytelling

D. *Anecdote*: a short account of a particular event or incident

E. *Authorities*: experts in a given field who offer specialized knowledge

On the line to the left of each example, write the letter of the matching term. Then, consult the answer key for the correct answers.

_______ 1. "Or your mood ring turns orange so you can climb into your Geo Metro and head to Wal-Mart for aspirin but instead find yourself reaching for St. John's wort." —Barcley Owens

_______ 2. "The moon is gently orange with a thin, star-white bottom; its dark top disappears into the blackness surrounding it." —Ed Bell

_______ 3. "Because of light pollution, some people have never seen a dark sky. 'In most cities, there's little point in gazing at the sky…unless you're fascinated by the sight of a few stars and some airplanes against a glowing background,' says David Tennenbaum, a science health and environment writer (ABCNEWS.com, *Technology Review, Bio-Science, Environmental Health Perspectives, American Health,* and other publications.)" —Ed Bell

_______ 4. Used as intellectual tools for developing, extending, and shaping ideas.

_______ 5. Martin Grove farmed the fields of northwestern Ohio for decades. He had fields of corn, wheat, and soybeans, and he developed a healthy orchard of apples…the best around, according to locals. In fact, in the summer of '68, Jerry Foster announced at the town jubilee that, next to Grove's apples, his own apples were fit for birds only. (And some say that the old saying, "that's for the birds," comes from Foster's proclamation.)

© 2013 Cengage Learning. All Rights Reserved. May not be scanned, copied or duplicated, or posted to a publicly accessible website, in whole or in part.

III. Writing Activity: Identifying Criteria

Researchers in everyday life establish criteria in numerous situations to narrow their research, to serve as guidelines for selection, and to aid in decision-making. Several lists of criteria used by prominent organizations follow below. Circle the numbers of the three most significant criteria, in your opinion, in each list. Then explain your reasons in the space that follows each list. If required, submit your responses to your instructor for evaluation.

1. ERIC (Education Resources Information Center) Selection Policy
   Materials selected for the ERIC databases are used by schools, institutions of higher education, educators, parents, administrators, policymakers, researchers, public and private entities, and the general public.

   List of Criteria for Selection of Materials:

   A. Relevance to education

   B. Quality guidelines (completeness, integrity, objectivity, substantive merit, utility/importance)

   C. Sponsorship by professional societies and organizations (national or international), and state or federal government agencies.

   D. Editorial/peer-review processes: adherence to ethical guidelines, fidelity to editorial conventions, methods of selection, procedure for retractions, opportunity for comments/opinions, publication history, reprint availability, scholarly review board, selectivity.

   Reasons: _____

   _____

   _____

   _____

   _____

   _____

   _____

   _____

   _____

   _____

   _____

   _____

   _____

2. Great Web Sites for Kids

   Criteria are used by the Association for Library Service to Children to select appropriate websites. Children are defined as persons of ages up to and including fourteen.

   List of Criteria for Selection of Websites:

   A. Authorship/sponsorship: Who put up the site?

   B. Purpose: What is its reason for being there?

   C. Design and stability: How easy is it to find and use the site?

   D. Content: Is the content meaningful and useful? Does it educate, inform, or entertain?

   Reasons: _____

   _____

   _____

   _____

   _____

   _____

   _____

   _____

   _____

   _____

   _____

   _____

   _____

   _____

   _____

   _____

   _____

   _____

   _____

3. University of California Digital Collection

Criteria guide librarians in selecting collections of analog materials for conversion to digital format and evaluating the benefits of digital versions.

List of Criteria for Selection of Materials:

A. Collection development: Does it meet information needs of faculty, students, and scholars?

B. Preservation/archiving: How high is the risk of losing the material if it is not digitized?

C. Access: Will it be deliverable through networked environments in use by the library community?

D. Organizational/funding: Does it add prestige to the institution?

Reasons: _____

_____

_____

_____

_____

_____

_____

_____

_____

_____

_____

_____

_____

_____

_____

_____

_____

_____

_____

_____

_____

Lesson 1—Everyday Research

9

4. The Schwab Foundation Network Entrepreneurs

Characteristics are evaluated by the Schwab Foundation to select a "Social Entrepreneur of the Year" and other entrepreneurs who will be included in the global Schwab Foundation Network. Social entrepreneurs can work in the fields of health, education, environment, micro-finance, and enterprise.

List of Criteria for Selection of Entrepreneurs:

A. Innovation: What social change has the candidate brought about?

B. Reach and scope: Has the initiative been expanded to other settings?

C. Replicability: Is the candidate openly sharing tools, techniques, and approaches to adapt the initiative to other settings?

D. Sustainability: Is the candidate dedicated to securing funds to continue the initiative?

E. Direct positive social impact: Are the benefits to the initiative clear and well documented?

F. Role model: Is the integrity of the candidate unquestionable?

G. Mutual value-added: Is the candidate willing to actively participate and support other entrepreneurs in the network?

Reasons: _____

_____

_____

_____

_____

_____

_____

_____

_____

_____

_____

_____

_____

_____

_____

_____

Lesson 1—Everyday Research

10

5. The Educator's Reference Desk™ Lesson Plan Collection:
   General criteria are used for selecting curriculum materials for a collection of more than 200 lesson plans submitted by teachers all over the world. The collection includes lesson plans on a variety of subjects for all grade levels.

   List of Criteria for Selection of Materials:

   A. Organization: Do materials include required elements that are easy to use?

   B. Educational objectives: Are materials clear and appropriate for grade level?

   C. Content: Do the materials have complete information and follow a logical development of ideas?

   D. Teaching strategies: Are materials and learning styles appropriate for age?

   E. Activities: Are materials related to objectives and are they relevant to students?

   F. Stereotyping, bias, and social inequity (selection should be sensitive to extremes): Do materials promote appreciation of diversity?

   G. Suitability of materials for learners: Are vocabulary and concepts used in the materials appropriate for age and student experience?

   H. Completeness: Do materials include bibliography and all required handouts?

   Reasons: _____

   _____

   _____

   _____

   _____

   _____

   _____

   _____

   _____

   _____

   _____

   _____

   _____

   _____

   _____

   _____

_____

ANSWER KEY

	Learning	Focus	
Answer	Objectives	Points	References

I. Writing Activity: Invention
.................LO 1 ....FP 2, 5, 7 .... video segment 3; textbook, pp. xxvii–xxx
(Your instructor will advise you about evaluating this assignment.)

II. Writing Activity: Chapter 1: Reading Argument
1. B.......LO 4 ....FP 1 ....textbook, pp. 37–38
2. C.......LO 4 ....FP 1, 3 .... video segments 1, 3, 4
3. E.......LO 4 ....FP 1 ....textbook, pp. 32–33
4. A.......LO 4 ....FP 1 ....textbook, pp. 10–11
5. D.......LO 4 ....FP 1 ....textbook, p. 38

III. Writing Activity: Identifying Criteria
.................LO 1 ....FP 2, 5 .... video segments 1, 2
(Your instructor will advise you about evaluating this assignment.)

Lesson 2

The Elements of Argument

The past is not a package one can lay away.

—Emily Dickinson

THEME

To apply the elements of argument, this lesson asks you to look at the past through the lens of a basic rhetorical argument. You will look at an unresolved event from the past, view it in a present perspective, and explore the connection between the past and present to argue for the resolution of the difference.

After you write an arguable thesis to make a claim about the past, you will develop your argument using support strategies like testimony, examples, authorities, and analogy. As you use these tools to build your argument, also consider using counterargument, concession, and qualifiers to make it strong and sturdy. When you argue about an unresolved event in the past equipped with rhetorical tools and your knowledge of the present, hopefully you will find that the experience strengthens your memory and reveals an insight that readers can relate to everyday life.

The past is our definition. We may strive, with good reason, to escape it, or to escape what is bad in it, but we will escape it only by adding something better to it.

—Wendell Berry

LESSON RESOURCES

Textbook: Mauk and Metz, *Inventing Arguments*
- Chapter 11, "Arguing the Past," pp. 283–321

Review:
- Chapter 2, "Claims," pp. 16–29
- Chapter 3, "Support," pp. 30–63
- Chapter 4, "Opposition," pp. 64–75

Video: "The Elements of Argument" from the series *The Writer's Odyssey*

LESSON GOAL

You will use the basic elements of argument to present a resolution of conflicting perspectives about a past event.

LESSON LEARNING OBJECTIVES

1. Identify the elements of a formal argument.

2. Write an arguable thesis that makes a claim or set of claims about the past.

3. Develop a variety of support strategies for an argument about something that is unresolved in the past.

4. Use suggestions from peers to improve the argument and counterarguments, concessions, and qualifiers.

LESSON FOCUS POINTS

1. What is inference? Line of reasoning?

2. Define the three types of reasoning: deductive, inductive, and analogical.

3. What are syllogisms? Enthymemes?

4. What are the differences between deductive and inductive reasoning?

5. What are metaphors?

6. Define each of the common logical fallacies: *ad hominem*, *straw person*, *post hoc*, *either/or*, *hasty generalizations*, *non sequitur*, *slippery slope*, *begging the question*, *red herring*, *bandwagon*, and *association*.

7. Discuss the six components of Toulminian Logic: claim, support, warranting assumption, backing, modal qualifier, and rebuttal.

8. How does a writer analyze the details of the past to write about an unresolved event? How does the event connect to general principles and precedents?

9. How do informal surveys assist in writing about an unresolved event from the past?

Lesson 2—The Elements of Argument

14

10. How does secondary research enable a writer to find a direction for the argument about the past?

11. What are cause/effect arguments? What are definition arguments? What are evaluation arguments? How can each of the above enhance the thesis of an argument about an unresolved event from the past?

12. What are clichés? Why should clichés be avoided in writing arguments?

13. How can an argumentative thesis be narrowed?

14. What is testimony? What are examples? Authorities? How can each support an argument about an unresolved event from the past?

15. What are analogies? Appeals to logic? Appeals to emotion? Appeals to value? Appeals to character? Appeals to need?

16. What are counterarguments? Concessions? Qualifiers? How can each support an argument about an unresolved event from the past?

17. How should a writer begin an argument about an unresolved event from the past? Where and how should a writer detail the past? Where should a writer explain other accounts of the past? Should a writer detail mainstream accounts?

18. What is common ground? How does a writer discover common ground?

19. What is elevated language? How does a writer use elevated language?

20. What is authority? How does a writer use authority?

21. What is irony? When is it appropriate to use irony in an argument?

22. Why is it useful to see the "final" essay as a rough draft?

WRITERS INTERVIEWED

James Ragland, Columnist, *The Dallas Morning News,* Dallas, TX

Gretchen Sween, Attorney and Writer, Susman Godfrey, LLP, Dallas, TX

SUGGESTED WRITING ASSIGNMENTS

Consult with your instructor and the course syllabus about requirements for any of the assignments listed below.

1. Explore an unresolved past event by connecting it to the present. Write an argumentative essay about the resolution of a past event.

2. Conduct a survey about your unresolved past event. Ask at least five people what they know about your topic. Ask them to give their accounts and opinions of what happened and how they characterized the events. Record their responses and write a summary of your findings.

> *The past is but the beginning of a beginning, and all that is or has been is but the twilight of the dawn.*
>
> —H. G. Wells

ENRICHMENT ACTIVITIES

Complete the following activities. An answer key and/or guidelines appear at the end of this lesson for each activity.

I. **Writing Activity: Arguable Thesis Statements**
    An arguable thesis statement is essential to any good argument. But, what is arguable? Arguable thesis statements make assertions that could be challenged on various grounds. They invite or directly address opposition.

    Pitfalls to avoid in writing a thesis statement include:

    ● Asking a question in your thesis

    ● Stating an obvious fact or widely held belief

    ● Declaring your personal likes or dislikes about a topic

    Review the thesis statements below. Based on the criteria described above, if the statement is arguable, put a YES on the line provided. If it is not arguable, write NO on the line provided. Rewrite each statement you believe is not arguable in the space below the statement. If required, submit your responses to your instructor for evaluation.

    _____ 1. The fact that we seem to want Shakespeare to have taken drugs for sensational value says more about our age of celebrity than it does about the great playwright.

_____ 2. So much suffering is caused or increased unnecessarily by America's urge to conquer.

_____ 3. When school funding does not keep up with the growing needs of students, the whole community pays the price.

_____ 4. People should avoid large corporate retailers.

_____ 5. The colonists were wrong in driving out the Native Americans.

_____ 6. There are many good things about public television.

_____ 7. Freedom, according to the song, is just another word for nothing left to lose, and now the best and brightest of women finally have something to lose.

_____ 8. Then the coal company came with the world's largest shovel and they tortured the timber and stripped all the land. Well, they dug for their coal till the land was forsaken, then they wrote it all down as the progress of man.

_____ 9. A guaranteed annual income makes as much economic sense now as it did in 1967, and far more sense than journeys to outer space.

_____ 10. The Civil War was sparked not by the flare of a cannon but by a flair for language.

II. **Writing Activity: Testimony, Examples, Authorities, and Analogy**
Support for your arguable thesis statement comes from a variety of choices. Your text suggests that you use some of the following support strategies:

- Testimony

- Examples

- Authorities

- Analogy

Listed below are five arguable thesis statements. Write at least one supporting statement for each arguable thesis using the strategies listed above. Identify the strategy (listed above) and provide an example in the spaces provided below each statement. If required, submit your responses to your instructor for evaluation.

Lesson 2—The Elements of Argument

17

1. Though we might prefer not to hear them, we can better understand who we are and why by taking in family stories as children.

   Support strategy: _____

   Example: _____

   _____

   _____

   _____

   _____

   _____

   _____

   _____

   _____

   _____

   _____

2. Stem cell research has prompted a complex marriage of law and biology that will continue to impact careers in both fields.

   Support strategy: _____

   Example: _____

   _____

   _____

   _____

   _____

   _____

   _____

   _____

   _____

   _____

   _____

Lesson 2—The Elements of Argument

3. Although college is often portrayed as a time of intense socializing and camaraderie, the students at Beach Community College suggest that it can be a solitary experience.

Support strategy: _____

Example: _____

_____

_____

_____

_____

_____

_____

_____

_____

_____

_____

4. Although numbers of people sometimes do conspire together, what some call a conspiracy is, in truth, various people with a similar attitude acting independently in their own self-interests.

Support strategy: _____

Example: _____

_____

_____

_____

_____

_____

_____

_____

_____

_____

_____

_____

_____

Lesson 2—The Elements of Argument

19

5. Despite the attraction of living away from home and experiencing life in unfamiliar territory, college students do benefit from living at home while attending school.

Support strategy: _____

Example: _____

_____

_____

_____

_____

_____

_____

_____

_____

_____

_____

III. Writing Activity: Revision Strategies

Revision is the key to successful writing. After several drafts of your essay, and when you are satisfied with the results, it is time to revise the essay as a complete piece of writing.

Excerpts from Mitch's draft of his essay in the lesson video are shown below. Evaluate these excerpts using the revision steps described in your textbook on pp. 320–321. Try to address each area when you look at Mitch's essay. Then, write a brief essay explaining what you suggest or even rewriting passages of the essay to assist Mitch in writing his final draft. If required, submit your responses to your instructor for evaluation.

Mitch's Draft

Asthma rates are soaring in the United States, and asthma-related health care costs are now in the billions. Take the case of Troy Marchant, a 10-year old boy who struggles just to play outside, while his mother struggles to pay his medical bills.

Who pays these costs? Insurance companies do, families do, and children do. Children pay when they have to give up outdoor activities, spend time in the hospital, miss school, and live attached to inhalers. Employers pay, in absenteeism and lost productivity when their employees are too sick to come to work. The government pays, when it funds Medicaid and other programs that help the poor cover medical costs.

The reason we tolerate such high levels of pollution is that there's no direct economic incentive for us to decrease our pollution. Simply put, we don't have to pay for it directly, and we don't understand what it's really costing us. What is the cost when beauty is lost? What is the cost when thousands of species of plants and animals, many that we haven't even discovered yet, are lost?

When damage to health and environmental destruction aren't factored into the price of doing business, we get artificially low prices, and corporations make big profits. But everyone loses. "We have always known that heedless self-interest was bad morals; now we know that it is bad economics." Obviously, we need a way to make consumers and corporations accountable. We need to pay directly for the right to pollute, or we will pollute ourselves out of existence.

When you purchase a TerraPass, you offset the emissions you create by sponsoring a decrease in emissions somewhere else. Carbon offset programs like TerraPass reduce the impact of the greenhouse gases that your daily activities put into the atmosphere, by using your money to support energy efficiency and renewable energy sources.

As environmental economists focus on ways to assign costs for pollution and create accountability for them, other ideas will emerge. The important thing is that we break through our denial, and recognize the true costs of our consumption habits.

ANSWER KEY

Answer	Learning Objectives	Focus Points	References

I. Writing Activity: Arguable Thesis Statement
1. Yes...........LO 2 ....FP 5 .... video segments 1, 2, 3; textbook, pp. 21–23, 307–308
2. Yes...........LO 2 ....FP 5 .... video segments 1, 2, 3; textbook, pp. 21–23, 307–308
3. Yes...........LO 2 ....FP 5 .... video segments 1, 2, 3; textbook, pp. 21–23, 307–308
4. No...........LO 2 ....FP 5 .... video segments 1, 2, 3; textbook, pp. 21–23, 307–308
5. No...........LO 2 ....FP 5 .... video segments 1, 2, 3; textbook, pp. 21–23, 307–308
6. No ....LO 2 ....FP 5 .... video segments 1, 2, 3; textbook, pp. 21–23, 307–308
7. Yes...........LO 2 ....FP 5 .... video segments 1, 2, 3; textbook, pp. 21–23, 307–308
8. Yes...........LO 2 ....FP 5 .... video segments 1, 2, 3; textbook, pp. 21–23, 307–308
9. Yes...........LO 2 ....FP 5 .... video segments 1, 2, 3; textbook, pp. 21–23, 307–308
10. Yes...........LO 2 ....FP 5 .... video segments 1, 2, 3; textbook, pp. 21–23, 307–308

II. Writing Activity: Testimony, Examples, Authorities, and Analogies
...............LO 1, 3 ....FP 6, 7, 12 .... video segments 1, 3, 4; textbook, pp. 310–311
(Your instructor will advise you about evaluating this assignment.)

III. Writing Activity: Revision Strategies
.................LO 4 ....FP 4–14 ....video segment 6; textbook, p. 320
(Your instructor will advise you about evaluating this assignment.)

Lesson 3

Refining a Thesis

Sometimes, a thesis sentence should resemble a famous quote. Just like famous words by Mark Twain, the thesis sentence should intrigue a reader with its clever composition and promise of things to come.

—Grace Fleming

THEME

In this lesson, you will focus on refining a thesis about the beginning or origin of something in terms of present ideas, events, and phenomena. Too often, we writers neglect to remember the origin of an event, or we do not go back to the beginning of something in order to place that event in perspective. You as a writer might compare yourself to an "explorer" looking into the mysteries of where something began. You will, hopefully, find hidden meaning as you explore your topic and refine your thesis. Refining your thesis is at the heart of this lesson, so as you write the different iterations of your thesis, you will discover the depth of your topic about origins.

Moments of origin (why, when, or how something began) are important. In accepting how something has started, you, the writer can also accept what can happen, what should happen, who or what should be involved, who or what should be excluded, and how the story is likely to end.

For this lesson, you will explore the origin of your topic, refine various iterations of your working thesis, and develop an argument. The arrangement of your argument will explore various kinds of support in evidence and appeals. In addition, you will pay close attention to your audience and your writer's voice. As you complete the lesson, the revision process will once again assist you as you look at the development and support of your thesis. Enjoy your journey into the mysteries of the beginnings of an idea, event, concept, or thing.

First comes thought; then organization of that thought, into ideas and plans; then transformation of those plans into reality. The beginning, as you will observe, is in your imagination.

—Napoleon Hill

Lesson 3—Refining a Thesis

23

LESSON RESOURCES

Textbook: Mauk and Metz: *Inventing Arguments*
- Chapter 7, "Arguing Definitions," pp. 129–167
- Chapter 8, "Arguing Causes," pp. 169–205

Review:
- Chapter 1, "Inventing Arguments," pp. 3–15
- Chapter 2, "Claims," pp. 16–29
- Chapter 3, "Support," pp. 30–63
- Chapter 11, "Arguing the Past," pp. 283–321

Video: "Refining a Thesis" from the series *The Writer's Odyssey*

> *No river can return to its source, yet all rivers must have a beginning.*
> —Native American Proverb

LESSON GOAL

You will develop a thesis that communicates why the origin of something matters and how it affects people's thoughts and lives.

LESSON LEARNING OBJECTIVES

1. Describe the function of a thesis statement in an argument.

2. Develop an arguable, focused and revelatory thesis.

3. Recognize how ideas evolve by examining the various iterations of the thesis for an argument.

4. Identify strategies for supporting an arguable thesis.

5. Develop self-evaluation skills.

LESSON FOCUS POINTS

1. How does a writer analyze the origin of ideas, events, or phenomena?

2. How does a writer develop an arguable thesis?

3. What parts do primary and secondary research play in supporting an arguable thesis?

4. Why should a writer argue about the significance of the origin of something?

5. What are ways a writer can develop support? Why are scenarios helpful as support for an argument?

6. Why do authorities present valuable information in an argumentative essay about origin?

7. How do appeals to logic assist the writer? How do appeals to value assist the writer?

8. What is the best line of reasoning to adopt in an argumentative essay about origin?

9. Why are counterarguments, concessions, and qualifiers important to address?

10. How should a writer begin an argumentative essay about origin? Where should the writer first discuss the subject of origin?

11. How does a writer separate evidence and appeals? How should a writer conclude an essay about origin?

12. How does a writer engage an audience through voice?

13. When should a writer use formal (informal) language? How are asides helpful? How do analogies assist a writer?

14. Why is the revision process necessary in an argumentative essay about origin?

15. How does a writer find common ground?

16. What are the qualities of an academic audience?

17. What is Rogerian argument?

18. What is sentence variety and how does it aid the writer's voice?

19. What are the differences between first, second, and third person reference in academic essay writing?

20. How does figurative language enhance a writer's voice?

21. Why is it important for a writer to avoid clichés?

22. What are "quiet connections"? What is exigence?

Lesson 3—Refining a Thesis

25

WRITERS INTERVIEWED

Ben Fong-Torres, Journalist, San Francisco, CA

James Ragland, Columnist, *The Dallas Morning News,* Dallas, TX

Robert Rivard, Editor, *The San Antonio Express-News,* San Antonio, TX

Richard Rodriquez, Essayist and Journalist, San Francisco, CA

SUGGESTED WRITING ASSIGNMENTS

Consult with your instructor and the course syllabus about requirements for any of the assignments listed below.

1. Write an argumentative essay about the origins of an idea, a concept, policy, event, phenomena, or belief. Your thesis should present unconventional thinking about the origin of the idea, concept, policy, event, phenomena, or belief.

> *With the possible exception of the equator, everything begins somewhere.*
> — Peter Robert Fleming

ENRICHMENT ACTIVITIES

Complete the following activities. An answer key and/or guidelines appear at the end of this lesson for each activity.

I. Writing Activity: Narrowing a Thesis
Writing a clear, focused, arguable thesis statement is essential when you discover the origin of something. Review each topic listed below and write four iterations of each thesis as you dig deeper into its origins. Make sure your final refined thesis is both arguable and relevant. If required, submit your responses to your instructor for evaluation.

1. Baseball, a world-famous sport, had its beginnings in America.

Iteration: _____

_____

_____

_____

_____

Lesson 3—Refining a Thesis

26

Iteration: _____

_____

_____

_____

_____

Iteration: _____

_____

_____

_____

_____

Refined Thesis: _____

_____

_____

_____

_____

2. Reality television shows began with "Candid Camera" and evolved into shows like "Survivor" and "Trading Spouses."

Iteration: _____

_____

_____

_____

_____

Iteration: _____

_____

_____

_____

_____

Iteration: _____

_____

_____

_____

_____

Lesson 3—Refining a Thesis

Refined Thesis: _____

_____

_____

_____

_____

II. Writing Activity: Primary and Secondary Support

Review pp. 31–36 in your textbook. Develop ways to support each refined thesis you developed in the exercise above.

For each refined thesis statement, give one example of a primary source you could use. If you interview someone, whom would you interview? If you do a survey, whom would you survey?

For each refined thesis statement, give one example of a secondary source you could use. Using Boolean operators (p. 383), look up secondary sources in a periodical database or Google, using the terms *origin beginning baseball* or *origin beginning reality show*. In the space provided, list one of the sources you found.

If required, submit your responses to your instructor for evaluation.

1. Refined thesis statement:

_____

_____

_____

_____

_____

_____

_____

_____

_____

_____

_____

_____

_____

Lesson 3—Refining a Thesis

Primary source:

_____

_____

_____

_____

_____

Secondary source:

_____

_____

_____

_____

_____

2. Refined thesis statement:

_____

_____

_____

_____

_____

Primary source:

_____

_____

_____

_____

_____

Secondary source:

_____

_____

_____

_____

_____

Lesson 3—Refining a Thesis

29

III. Writing Activity: Using Appeals to Logic and Value

Review the information about appeals in your textbook in Chapter 3, pp. 43–56. Pay particular attention to the examples of appeals to logic and value. To support the refined thesis statements you developed in Writing Activity I, describe at least one appeal to logic and one appeal to value. Be specific about the appeal. Exactly what wording might you use to appeal to the logic or values of your chosen audience in supporting your refined thesis? List the refined thesis and the two appeals in the space provided. If required, submit your responses to your instructor for evaluation.

1. Refined thesis (baseball):

_____

_____

_____

_____

_____

_____

_____

_____

_____

_____

Appeal to logic:

_____

_____

_____

_____

Appeal to value:

_____

_____

_____

_____

_____

2. Refined thesis (Reality Shows):

_____

_____

_____

_____

_____

Primary source:

_____

_____

_____

_____

Secondary source:

_____

_____

_____

_____

_____

ANSWER KEY

Answer	Learning Objectives	Focus Points	References

I. Writing Activity: Narrowing a Thesis
..............LO 1, 2, 3...............FP 2... video segments 1, 3, 5
(Your instructor will advise you about evaluating this assignment.)

II. Writing Activity: Primary and Secondary Sources
.................LO 4..................FP 3, 5..textbook, pp. 363–383
(Your instructor will advise you about evaluating this assignment.)

III. Writing Activity: Using Appeals to Logic and Value
.................LO 4...............FP 5, 7, 11...textbook, pp. 43–56
(Your instructor will advise you about evaluating this assignment.)

Lesson 4

Building Support

One must be drenched in words, literally soaked in them, to have the right ones form themselves into the proper pattern at the right moment.

—Hart Crane

THEME

Developing relevant and timely support is crucial to writing a good argument. In this lesson, you will learn to create a convincing argument about a particular definition by supporting that definition with a variety of rhetorical strategies.

Students are often curious about the world around them and are attentive to definitions, particularly dictionary definitions. However, they often ignore fundamental qualities by not seeking out all possibilities of an object or idea or belief. Pursuing these possibilities would take them far beyond the dictionary definition of something important in their majors or their lives to discover "the meaning behind the meaning."

Arguments over definitions arise when the term or idea has many layers or dimensions. Your argument should reflect the support strategies of evidence, examples, and appeals to delineate your definition. As you argue for your definition, you will also need to incorporate counterarguments, qualifiers, and concessions. Pursue your definition and argue passionately for it with the tools presented in this lesson.

Like stones, words are laborious and unforgiving, and the fitting of them together, like the fitting of stones, demands great patience and strength of purpose and particular skill.

—Edmund Morrison

LESSON RESOURCES

Textbook: Mauk and Metz: *Inventing Arguments*
- Chapter 5, "Hidden Layers," pp. 77–95
- Chapter 6, "Analyzing Argument," pp. 97–125

Review:
- Chapter 7, "Arguing Definitions," pp. 129 –167

Video: "Building Support" from the series *The Writer's Odyssey*

Writing became such a process of discovery that I couldn't wait to get to work in the morning: I wanted to know what I was going to say.

—Sharon O'Brien

LESSON GOAL

You will communicate a convincing argument that explores definitions using a variety of rhetorical strategies to discover "the meaning behind the meaning."

LESSON LEARNING OBJECTIVES

1. Combine research and original thinking to discover the fundamental qualities of a subject.

2. Develop evidence, examples, and appeals to support an argument.

3. Incorporate counterarguments, qualifiers, and concessions into the argument strategy.

4. Engage in peer revision of a draft of an essay to assess the effectiveness of the support used in the essay.

I would hurl words into this darkness and wait for an echo, and if an echo sounded, no matter how faintly, I would send other words to tell, to march, to fight, to create a sense of hunger for life that gnaws in us all.

—Richard Wright

LESSON FOCUS POINTS

1. What is invention? How might a writer explore the boundaries of a term?

2. What is the most important debate being waged in your community and how might that knowledge be helpful to you as a writer of a definition argument? What is an important cultural or national debate and why is that helpful in defining a term?

3. In analyzing a situation, why should a writer know what people normally think of when they hear the term? Why should a writer know why people might disagree or agree about the term? Why should a writer know what an appropriate definition might be and how to define the topic correctly?

4. How are surveys helpful in a definition argument? How can researching external sources be helpful in a definition argument?

Lesson 4—Building Support

34

5. How can periodical databases be useful in a definition argument? How about newspaper databases?

6. How can the Internet be helpful? Why should writers use caution when using the Internet as a source?

7. Why should the opposite meanings of a term be useful in a definition argument?

8. Why is a narrow, arguable thesis important in a definition argument?

9. What are ways to develop support for an argument? How are examples, scenarios, allusions, and testimony useful?

10. What about appeals to logic, emotion, value? How are appeals helpful?

11. How are counterarguments and concessions helpful in an argument of definition? Is it necessary for a concession to go in every argument?

12. How should a writer begin an argument of definition? Where should the definition appear in the arrangement of the argument?

13. Why is a specific audience important in a definition argument?

14. How can voice strengthen a definition argument? What is formality? What is informality?

15. How might a writer revise a definition argument? How might a writer determine if the situation and its details are thorough enough for a definition argument?

WRITERS INTERVIEWED

Gretchen Sween, Attorney and Writer, Susman Godfrey, LLP, Dallas, TX

Mike Trimble, Opinion Page Editor, *Denton Record-Chronicle,* Denton, TX

James Ragland, Columnist, *The Dallas Morning News,* Dallas, TX

SUGGESTED WRITING ASSIGNMENTS

1. Write an argumentative essay of definition for a specific audience in your classroom, your work place, or your community using a variety of rhetorical strategies.

2. Create a line of reasoning that would allow an audience to accept the following definitions. To create a line of reasoning, ask yourself: What basic points (or premises) must someone believe in order to accept the definition?

- Freedom: the state in which people are able to choose what they should do.

- Education: the processes of learning how to learn.

- Politics: the art of what is possible.

> *Don't try to figure out what other people want to hear from you; figure out what you have to say. It's the one and only thing you have to offer.*
> —Barbara Kingsolver

ENRICHMENT ACTIVITIES

Complete the following activities. An answer key and/or guidelines appear at the end of this lesson for each activity.

I. **Writing Activity: Counterarguments, Concessions, Qualifiers**
Counterarguments, concessions, and qualifiers assist you, the writer, in bolstering your argument. Your readers view you as objective and thorough because you look beyond your own argument to see what the other side points out.

Briefly, *counterarguments* refute claims or positions opposed to those being forwarded by the writer. *Concessions* acknowledge the value of other or opposing positions. *Qualifiers* acknowledge the limits of one's claims.

For this exercise, identify each statement below as a counterargument, concession, or qualifier. (All passages are from the textbook.) Use the blank to the left for your response. Compare your answers to the key shown at the end of the lesson.

_____ 1. But this is not true because there have been differences between their moralities, but these have never amounted to anything like a total difference.

_____ 2. I agree with you that people should be able to figure some things out. Some people will be able to figure out more than others.

_____ 3. However, this is just wrong. Americans should be paid well because they do a great job.

_____ 4. But this is not an anti-hunting essay or an anti-house-in-the-wilderness essay. It is an anti-big-house-in-the-wilderness essay.

_____ 5. Women are hardwired to experience and recall emotions more readily than men, according to a study announced last month in the *Proceedings of the National Academy of Sciences,* as well as on CNN's morning show.

_____ 6. Maybe I've set the bar too low, but I found this tied score heartening considering that only seven percent of survey respondents said that they had lost important rights and liberties of their own to the war against terrorism.

II. Writing Activity: The Oxford English Dictionary

If you are truly interested in the etymology of a term or a word, the best source for historical and usage information through time for any word in the English language is the *Oxford English Dictionary (OED)* in your college library. "The *OED* is the accepted authority on the evolution of the English language over the last millennium. It is a guide to the meaning, history, and pronunciation of over half a million words, both present and past. It traces the usage of words through 2.5 million quotations from a wide range of international English language sources, from classic literature and specialist periodicals to film scripts and cookery books" (Oxford University Press).

Select two words from the list below. Look both words up in *The Oxford English Dictionary.* Trace the history of their usage through time. Then write a letter to your instructor or to a friend explaining your findings and your reactions to each word. Will your findings make a difference in the way you use the words in the future? Do you have a better understanding of where the words came from? Will you incorporate an earlier meaning of the words into your own vocabulary? Use a conversational tone in your letter. If required, submit your responses to your instructor for evaluation.

WORD CHOICES:

amazement	ardor	embrace
bitterness	beauty	joy

III. Writing Activity: Revision

In the video for this lesson, "Building Support," Jada drafts an essay about the meaning of family. Review her essay printed below and answer the following questions.

1. What support strategies does she use to support her thesis (examples, scenarios, authorities, etc.), and why is each necessary and effective?

2. What appeals do you think are important to her argument and why? Did she include all appeals that you would if you were writing about family?

3. Reread Jada's argument carefully. Where does she counterargue, concede, and qualify her argument? Where would you counterargue, concede, and qualify your argument if you were writing about the meaning of family?

4. How might Jada rearrange her argument for her reader? What additional words, phrases, and sentences would help connect ideas for her reader?

5. Examine Jada's voice. Point out where Jada's voice might alienate the reader. Make suggestions to her to draw the reader in.

If required, submit your responses to your instructor for evaluation.

JADA'S ROUGH DRAFT

The AIDS orphan crisis constitutes the greatest social and human problem in the history of mankind. Literally millions of destitute children are now without parents, all due to the deadly spread of AIDS in sub-Saharan Africa, and millions more children will be orphaned in the next ten years without a real global effort. In order to respond to the AIDS orphan crisis, we Americans must expand our idea of family to include the whole world.

As of 2003, there were an estimated 15.2 million African children under 14 years old orphaned by HIV/AIDS, 1.8 million in Nigeria alone. By 2010 that number will rise to more than 18 million, and that is only the orphans in Africa. In some African countries the number of children orphaned by AIDS makes up half or more of all orphans nationally, including 78% in Zimbabwe and 77% in Botswana.

In America after the Civil War, black Americans rallied to rejoin families broken apart by slavery. While some families were successfully reconnected, many children never found their original parents and were taken in and raised by families barely able to support themselves. My grandmother's great grandmother was one of these motherless children, adopted and raised by a couple whose own children had been wrenched from them under the slave system.

If something isn't done the problem will only worsen. If left unchecked millions more people will die from this deadly disease, and we will be facing an orphan crisis far more severe than the one we have now. We have all viewed commercials for needy children on TV, and many of us have written checks to help, but it will take a larger commitment to ameliorate conditions for millions of defenseless children.

Current DNA research manifests that all human beings on the planet are closely related. In fact, it is estimated that all six billion of us are descended from a single group of only a few thousand humans who migrated out of Africa in the last 100,000 years. *The Oxford English Dictionary* defines family as "those descended, or claiming descent, from a common ancestor." Thus it is irrefutable that if we are indeed descended from a common ancestry, then these orphans really are part of our family, and we need to start behaving as if we are one.

"Not only does adopting internationally assist families in achieving their dream of parenthood, but it also fulfills the dream of children in orphanages and foster homes who await the love of a family." For the many childless Americans who long for parenthood, adopting an orphan can be, as the Chinese say, a double happiness. According to the Gladney Agency, which has recently pioneered an adoption program in Ethiopia, "Not only does adopting internationally assist families in achieving their dream of parenthood, but it also fulfills the dream of children in orphanages and foster homes who await the love of a family."

Granted, not everyone is in a position to raise a child. But for those who aren't prepared to be a mother or father to an orphan, there are plenty of ways to be a brother or sister, aunt or uncle, grandparent or godparent…

_____
_____
_____
_____
_____
_____
_____
_____
_____
_____

Lesson 4—Building Support

ANSWER KEY

I. Writing Activity: Counterarguments, Concessions, Qualifiers

Answer	Learning Objectives	Focus Points	References
1. Counterargument	LO 3	FP 11	video segments 5, 6; textbook, pp. 65–71
2. Concession	LO 3	FP 11	video segments 5,6; textbook, pp. 65–71
3. Counterargument	LO 3	FP 11	video segments 5,6; textbook, pp. 65–71
4. Qualifier	LO 3	FP 11	video segments 5,6; textbook, pp. 65–71
5. Qualifier	LO 3	FP 11	video segments 5,6; textbook, pp. 65–71
6. Concession	LO 3	FP 11	video segments 5,6; textbook, pp. 65–71

II. Writing Activity: *The Oxford English Dictionary*

	LO 1	FP 1	video segments 1, 2

(Your instructor will advise you about evaluating this assignment.)

III. Writing Activity: Revision

	LO 4	FP 15	video segment 4; textbook, pp. 166–167

(Your instructor will advise you about evaluating this assignment.)

Lesson 5

Voicing an Argument

To me, the greatest pleasure of writing is not what it's about, but the music the words make.

—Truman Capote

THEME

All human beings create their own voices in writing, speaking, and gesturing through their interaction with the world. Creating voice takes practice, particularly in an argument. In this lesson, you will practice using various rhetorical techniques such as arrangement, repetition, and sentence structure to create your voice. Skillful use of these techniques will then help you use your voice to deliver and emphasize to the audience a strong and cogent argument.

This lesson will also assist you in making meaning and arguing meaning. Meaning is a collective understanding of the world. Meaning is not always a matter of agreement. All things mean, and that meaning is always potentially different from what a thing's writer or creator may have intended. Meaning making is never a simple process. In writing an argument about the meaning of something, delve deeply into the meaning of the word or concept or idea. Then use rhetorical techniques to create a voice that convinces readers that your argument is worthy of their attention.

Being a writer means having homework the rest of your life.

—Lawrence Kasdan

LESSON RESOURCES

Textbook: Mauk and Metz: *Inventing Arguments*
- Chapter 15, "Men and Women," pp. 471–492

Review:
- Chapter 1, "Inventing Arguments," pp. 3–15
- Chapter 2, "Claims," pp. 16–29
- Chapter 3, "Support," pp. 30–63
- Chapter 4, "Opposition," pp. 64–75
- Chapter 5, "Hidden Layers," pp. 77–95
- Chapter 6, "Analyzing Argument," pp. 97–125
- Chapter 7, "Arguing Definitions," pp. 129–167

Video: "Voicing an Argument" from the series *The Writer's Odyssey*

LESSON GOAL

You will use a particular voice to explain the meaning of details and subtle links between a subject and the world.

LESSON LEARNING OBJECTIVES

1. Incorporate a variety of writing strategies in arranging the argument of meaning.

2. Explore techniques that establish a writer's voice in the argument of meaning.

LESSON FOCUS POINTS

1. What questions might you ask during the invention process to help you determine a topic for an argument about meaning?

2. How is considering the most important debate being waged in the community helpful in determining a topic for an argument about meaning? How is it helpful to determine what a particular thing means within a particular cultural situation? How is it helpful to consider what broader beliefs or values would influence the audience?

3. How may you gather outside perspectives on the meaning of a subject?

4. How do surveys and secondary research assist you in writing an argument about meaning?

5. How do you develop a thesis for an argumentative essay? How do you develop support?

6. What are allusions? What are definitions? What is personal testimony? What are authorities? How are each helpful in expanding a writer's voice?

7. How can appeals to logic and appeals to value assist a writer?

8. How are counterarguments, concessions, and qualifiers valuable?

9. How should you begin an argument about meaning? How should you integrate sources? How do you integrate quoted material?

10. What else might a writer do besides summarize in the conclusion of an argument about meaning?

11. Why is sentence structure an important tool in expressing your voice?

---

12. How do repeating structures help a writer express voice?

13. What are the best techniques a writer might use to express voice?

14. What is stasis theory? Explain conjecture, definition, quality, and procedure.

15. What is Hegelian logic? Explain thesis, antithesis, and synthesis.

WRITERS INTERVIEWED

Elizabeth Crook, Author and Novelist, Austin, TX

Macarena Hernandez, Editorial Columnist, *The Dallas Morning News,* Dallas, TX

Matt Zoller Seitz, Film and Television Critic, *New York Press/Newark Star-Ledger,* Brooklyn, NY

Judy Yung, Historian and Author, Santa Cruz, CA

SUGGESTED WRITING ASSIGNMENTS

1. Write an argumentative essay that expresses the underlying meaning of something in a particular voice.

2. Examine how banks and other institutions (your college, the telephone company, your DSL provider, etc.) argue about meaning. Select one institution and study its arguments. If studying your college, for example, you might visit the admissions office, notice its posters and advertising, review its catalogue, and review its website. Write a brief essay about the arguments you find and the voice used to communicate the argument.

A writer is someone who can make a riddle out of an answer.

—Karl Kraus

ENRICHMENT ACTIVITIES

Complete the following activities. An answer key and/or guidelines appear at the end of this lesson for each activity.

I. Writing Activity: Arrangement

Arranging your thoughts in an essay about meaning is crucial to the voice and tone of the argument. Review the discussion about "Arrangement" in your textbook on p. 162. Pay attention to how the writers begin, integrate sources, and conclude in the essays you read in the textbook chapter as well as other argumentative essays in newspapers, magazines, television documentaries, etc.

Select one of the readings from Chapter 15 in your textbook, "Men and Women," pp. 471–492. Read the essay carefully.

In a brief essay, dissect the writer's argument, paying attention to the way the writer begins, integrates sources, and concludes. Be as specific as possible in your responses, quoting passages that highlight your thoughts.

- How does the writer begin?

- Is the beginning effective? Does it create an expectation about its argument in you the reader?

- Does the writer include external sources to support the argument? How effective are the references in furthering the argument?

- Does the writer summarize in the conclusion, or does the writer find another means of bringing the argument home?

Overall, does the writer arrange the essay so that it strengthens the argument and the writer's voice? If required, submit your essay to your instructor for evaluation.

II. Writing Activity: Voice

The writer's voice prompts the reader to accept and embrace the argument in an essay of meaning, and there are numerous ways to manipulate one's voice. Two of the simplest ways to engage the audience and convince readers that the claims of the argument are reasonable are sentence structure and repeating structures.

Sentence structure can create a determined and intense feeling, or it can create a sense of reflection and intrigue. Alternating long and short sentences can create a lively voice. Good writers try to use sentences to guide readers through different patterns. Careful writers use sentence structure to diffuse a potentially harsh idea.

Repeating structures are often present when writers want to draw readers into a particular pattern of thinking. Repetition actually draws the reader into the way of thinking. Like the rhythm of a song, it drives the reader along, reinforcing ideas. Good writers use repetition to create an intellectual pulse.

Rewrite the passage below from Jada's essay. Vary the sentence structure and use repeating structures to amplify her voice and to bring her argument home. If required, submit your revision to your instructor for evaluation.

EXCERPT FROM JADA'S ESSAY

In many African countries, the family support system is gutted by AIDS. Children barely big enough to ride the roller coaster in America try to be moms and dads to their younger siblings. Grandparents and great-grandparents, aging and infirm, cannot cope with the needs of the young and abandoned. Who will step in to fill the gap? Granted, not everyone is in a position to raise a child. But for those who aren't prepared to be a mother or father to an orphan, there are plenty of ways to be a brother or sister, aunt or uncle, grandparent or godparent.

The *OED* tells us that family means 'those descended…from a common ancestor.' Our DNA tells us that everybody on the planet, all six billion of us, come from a single clan that lived in Africa during the last hundred thousand years. So we really are one big family, and it's way past time that we open our hearts and our minds to that reality.

So tell me, brothers and sisters: What are we going to do about the children?

ANSWER KEY

	Learning Objectives	Focus Points	References

I. Writing Activity: Arrangement
................LO 1.............FP 8, 13, 14.. video segments 3, 4; textbook, p. 162

II. Writing Activity: Voice
................LO 2..................FP 15...............................video segments 1, 3, 5, 6; textbook, pp. 471–492

Lesson 6

Gathering Research

Somewhere, something incredible is waiting to be known.
—Dr. Carl Sagan

THEME

In this lesson, you will discover how to gather information for a research project. While you are still a student, research techniques and writing research papers will more than likely be a great part of your courses. Once you leave the academic world, the research tools you gather here will benefit you in your daily life and in your working world.

In this lesson, you will discover the differences between primary and secondary research. Primary research allows you to find your own information through conducting interviews with a primary source, like the author of a book you are researching or Mitch's interview with an expert on endangered frogs in the video. Or you may wish to develop a survey to seek opinion about your topic, like Rosa's survey of church members in the video.

Secondary research allows you to find information for your research topic in books, periodicals, journals, newspapers, the Internet, and other sources. You will also become acquainted with online search engines that assist you in narrowing the secondary resources you will need for a specific topic.

You will discover that research is a process of discovery. You will gather information for your project, and if you carefully apply evaluative criteria to your sources, you will discover a wealth of information on your topic.

Research is formalized curiosity. It is poking and prying with a purpose.
—Zora Neale Hurston

LESSON RESOURCES

Textbook: Mauk and Metz: *Inventing Arguments*
- Chapter 13, "The Research Guide: Overview of Research" pp. 360–394
- Chapter 14, "Politics," pp. 455–469

Video: "Gathering Research" from the series *The Writer's Odyssey*

LESSON GOAL

You will be able to research a topic by locating information about the topic in a variety of credible sources.

LESSON LEARNING OBJECTIVES

1. Formulate a question that helps to narrow a topic for a research project.

2. Search for information in secondary sources such as books, journal articles, newspapers, the Internet, literary sources, etc.

3. Search for information on the topic by using primary sources of information.

4. Apply criteria for evaluating sources such as ideology, relevance, reliability, credibility, timeliness, and diversity to evaluate the sources for an argumentative research paper.

LESSON FOCUS POINTS

1. Why, when, and where should a writer find information from sources on a topic for a researched argument?

2. What is plagiarism? Why should you avoid plagiarism in an argumentative research paper?

3. Why should you document sources in writing a research paper? What is formal versus informal documentation?

4. Why should you be careful about websites?

5. What is the research path? What is inventive research? How does seeking research differ from inventive research? How are each helpful to you in writing a research paper?

6. How do you conduct primary research?

7. How are interviews helpful in conducting research? How do you compose interview questions for argumentative research? What are follow-up questions? How are they helpful in conducting research? What are the best ways to plan an interview? How do you use interviews in argumentative research?

---

8. How are surveys helpful to you in argumentative research? What are ways to generate survey questions? How do you choose survey respondents? How do you record survey responses? How do you use survey responses in argumentative research?

9. What are literary works? What are religious texts? How are both helpful in argumentative research?

10. How do you conduct secondary research for an argumentative research project?

11. What should you know about newspapers, magazines, journals? How do you tell the difference between magazines and journals?

12. What should you know about government documents, reference books, websites, blogs and chats, visual media?

13. What should you know about searching the library when doing argumentative research?

14. Why should a writer avoid using encyclopedias and *Wikipedia* in doing academic research?

WRITERS INTERVIEWED

Monika Antonelli, Reference Librarian, University of North Texas Libraries, Denton, TX

Hampton Sides, Author, Santa Fe, NM

Judy Yung, Historian and Author, Santa Cruz, CA

SUGGESTED WRITING ASSIGNMENT

Consult with your instructor and the course syllabus about requirements for the assignment listed below.

Formulate a question, search for information in primary and secondary sources, and take notes on the research for an argumentative research project.

> *It is important that students bring a certain ragamuffin, barefoot, irreverence to their studies; they are not here to worship what is known, but to question it.*
>
> —Jacob Bronowski

ENRICHMENT ACTIVITIES

Complete the following activities. An answer key and/or guidelines appear at the end of this lesson for each activity.

I. **Writing Activity: Selecting Secondary Sources**
Visit a college or university library, either physically or online, and locate appropriate secondary sources for one of the topics listed below. Try to include a variety of sources: books, journals, newspaper articles, and Internet sources. Access, if available, an online database for more specific information on the topic. List all information about the source: title, author, date of publication, place published, etc. If required, submit your responses to your instructor for evaluation.

Topics:
- Global warming
- Alternate energy sources
- The Green movement in building environment friendly edifices
- Oliver Wendell Holmes
- Reality television shows

II. **Writing Activity: Primary Sources**
Visit a college or university library, either physically or online, and locate appropriate primary sources for one of the topics listed below. As a researcher, try to locate as much information as possible by the primary source, particularly biographies, interviews, memberships, books, journal articles, and research studies. Access, if available, an online database for more specific information on the primary source. List all the information about the source: title, author, date of publication, place published, etc. If required, submit your responses to your instructor for evaluation.

Topics:
- Al Gore and global warming
- Edgar Allen Poe
- Oprah Winfrey
- Gallaudet University
- American Numismatist Society
- The Sierra Club

III. Writing Activity: Interviews and Surveys
For this activity, select either A or B.

A. Choose a potential topic for your research project. Develop interview questions following the guidelines in your text on pp. 363–366. Decide who you will interview, and gear your questions to the audience and the topic.

B. Choose a potential topic for your research project. Develop a survey following the guidelines in your text on pp. 372–373. Decide who you will survey, and gear your questions to the audience and the topic.

If required, submit your responses to your instructor for evaluation.

ANSWER KEY

Answer	Learning Objectives	Focus Points	References

I. Writing Activity: Selecting Secondary Sources
................LO 2..............FP 1, 10–13..video segment 1; textbook, pp. 374–383
(Your instructor will advise you about evaluating this assignment.)

II. Writing Activity: Primary Sources
................LO 3..............FP 1, 6–8..video segment 3; textbook, pp. 363–373
(Your instructor will advise you about evaluating this assignment.)

III. Writing Activity: Interviews and Surveys
................LO 3..............FP 1, 6–8..video segment 3; textbook, pp. 363–373
(Your instructor will advise you about evaluating this assignment.)

Lesson 7

Integrating Research

Writing is an exploration. You start from nothing and learn as you go.
—E. L. Doctorow

THEME

You have uncovered a multitude of facts, data, and evidence in numerous primary and secondary sources on a topic, so what next? Next, you discover an organized way of putting them all together, succinctly and logically. You are now at the point where you can organize your information in an outline or on a visual organizer. Once you figure out general topics and arrange your information within those topics, you can determine where you need more information or decide where you have too much information or identify an area you completely overlooked in finding sources.

After you have a planning document, you can begin writing your argumentative research essay. In this lesson, you will learn how to integrate your argumentative commentary with the arguments or counterarguments of your primary and secondary sources. You will practice the skills of directly quoting a source, paraphrasing a source, and summarizing a source so that you do not plagiarize. Avoiding plagiarism is of the utmost importance because you do not want to be accused of "stealing" someone else's words or ideas.

Once you start your draft, pay attention to the way you have integrated your sources. Try highlighting direct quotes, paraphrases, and summaries on a couple of pages. Check the highlighted passages to make certain you have included your own commentary and to make certain you have quoted, paraphrased, or summarized your sources appropriately, giving credit where it is due. Remember, integrating sources is a major part of the research process. Please allow yourself the extra time necessary to try various approaches.

Writing is just a process of connections.
—Raymond Carver

LESSON RESOURCES

Textbook: Mauk and Metz: *Inventing Arguments*
- Chapter 13, "The Research Guide: Integrating Sources," pp. 395–410
- Chapter 16, "Race," pp. 495–513

Video: "Integrating Research" from the series *The Writer's Odyssey*

LESSON GOAL

You will understand the techniques necessary to organize information from credible sources during the process of writing argumentative research and to integrate support sources internally.

LESSON LEARNING OBJECTIVES

1. Organize information from both primary and secondary sources to integrate into the planning document for a research project.

2. Integrate information from primary and secondary sources into the text of a draft of an argumentative research paper by quoting, paraphrasing, and summarizing.

3. Blend sources appropriately by framing the writer's thoughts and providing commentary about the information in an argumentative research paper.

LESSON FOCUS POINTS

1. What are ways you may use to integrate external sources in an argumentative research paper? How are outlines and visual maps used in integrating external sources?

2. What should you, as a writer, know about plagiarism?

3. How is paraphrase used in integrating sources?

4. How is summary used in integrating external sources in an argumentative research paper?

---

5. How are quotations used in integrating external sources? What are guidelines for quotations? What are the guidelines for punctuation in integrating external sources in an argumentative research paper?

6. How might a writer blend information from an external source?

7. How does a writer counterargue with external sources?

8. What are the best ways for a writer to use textual cues to distinguish the thinking of the writer from the thinking of the author of the external source?

9. Why are paragraph transitions important in integrating sources in an argumentative research paper?

WRITERS INTERVIEWED

Elizabeth Crook, Author and Novelist, Austin, TX

Judy Yung, Historian and Author, Santa Cruz, CA

SUGGESTED WRITING ASSIGNMENTS

Consult with your instructor and the course syllabus about requirements for any of the assignments listed below.

1. Write a draft of an argumentative research paper, integrating sources by quoting, paraphrasing, summarizing, and framing the writer's thoughts and commentary.

2. Complete the "Activity" on pages 398 and 400 of your textbook on paraphrasing and summary.

> *When something can be read without effort, great effort has gone into its writing.*
>
> —Enrique Jardiel Poncela

ENRICHMENT ACTIVITIES

Complete the following activities. An answer key and/or guidelines appear at the end of this lesson for each activity.

I. Writing Activity: Organizing Sources
In the video, authors Judy Yung, Historian, and Elizabeth Crook, Historical Novelist, describe their organizational structures.

> JUDY YUNG: I have this system where as I gather information and evidence and stories and materials, I put them in file folders by subject. And, as the folders get thicker and thicker, I divide them into other folders, and then I arrange all these folders in some way…maybe by period or subject matter. Then, when it comes to writing, I have everything already organized in a way, so I can find that information and all the information on similar topics is all together.

> ELIZABETH CROOK: It's a matter of really finding the information you want to use, then recording it, and then putting it in a place where you can come across it again. These file boxes provide examples of how I organize information by subject. Each file in each box includes photographs, maps, historical documents, letter, etc. Often, I would make notes on things that I wanted to use, but I would forget if it wasn't right there in my file.

Write a brief essay describing your organizational strategies. What do you think about the strategies that Judy Yung and Elizabeth Crook use to organize their historical information gathering? Are you willing to try either approach? Discuss their approaches in your essay also.

If required, submit your responses to your instructor for evaluation.

II. Writing Activity: Formal Outline vs. Spider Map
When you organize information before writing, it helps to develop an outline or to create a visual map.

A. When you write an outline, after you sort through primary and secondary sources, divide your subject into major topics, much like Rosa does in her outline about church sanctuary. Use the example below to develop an outline from your own topic. If necessary, write notes to yourself about items to check as you write your outline.

Example
Rosa's Outline: Church Sanctuary

OUTLINE

I. Introduction and Thesis

   A. Set-up: recent case in Chicago
      1) Church sanctuary for woman
      2) Numerous news articles   Note: Check news articles

   B. Explanation of Sanctuary
      1) Ancient tradition
      2) Controversial history

   C. Thesis statement: When churches feel entitled to break the law by offering sanctuary, they may do it to protect the innocent, but they are also providing shelter to the guilty.

_____

_____

_____

_____

_____

_____

_____

_____

_____

_____

_____

_____

_____

_____

_____

_____

_____

Lesson 7—Integrating Research

_____

_____

_____

_____

_____

_____

_____

_____

_____

_____

_____

_____

B. When you construct a spider map like Mitch's map in the video, you use a
graphic organizer to help you enumerate the various aspects of your topic. When
constructing a spider map, write your main topic in the circle, list the main ideas
on the extended legs, then list the details on the arms extending from each leg.
Complete a spider map about your topic using the example below. If required,
submit your responses to your instructor for evaluation.

Spider Map

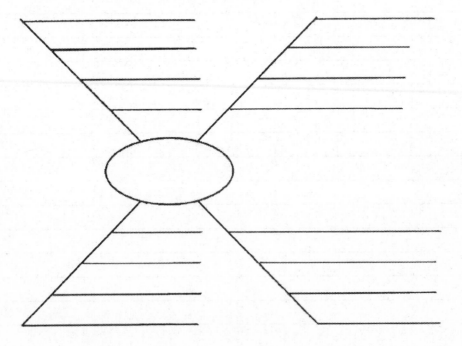

III. Writing Activity: Plagiarism

Review pp. 400–402 in your textbook. In your own words, define plagiarism. Then, explain in detail what consequences students might suffer if they plagiarize the work of someone else. What is the policy at your institution regarding plagiarism? What is your responsibility if you suspect other students of committing plagiarism? You will more than likely find this information in the published Student Code of Conduct for your college or university. Put all of your thoughts into a brief essay.

If required, submit your responses to your instructor for evaluation.

_____
_____
_____
_____
_____
_____
_____
_____
_____
_____
_____
_____
_____
_____
_____
_____
_____
_____
_____
_____
_____
_____
_____

_____

ANSWER KEY

Answer	Learning Objectives	Focus Points	References

I. Writing Activity: Organizing Sources
.................LO 1 ....FP 3, 4, 5, 6 ....video segment 3; textbook, pp. 395–410
(Your instructor will advise you about evaluating this assignment.)

II. Writing Activity: Formal Outline vs. Spider Map
.................LO 1 ....FP 1 .... video segments 1, 2
(Your instructor will advise you about evaluating this assignment.)

III. Writing Activity: Plagiarism
.................LO 2 ....FP 1, 2 ....video segment 3; textbook, pp. 400–402
(Your instructor will advise you about evaluating this assignment.)

Lesson 8

Documenting Research

Research is to see what everybody else has seen, and to think what nobody else has thought.

—Albert Szent-Gyorgyi

THEME

In this lesson, you will apply the techniques of documenting research in writing an effective argumentative paper. You will also learn about styles of documentation. What is the MLA format? Why would you use that format rather than the APA format? Either format is helpful to readers of your research because it provides them with specific information about your external sources. If a reader wants to locate a source to read it in its entirety, the list of sources presents all of the information the reader needs about the author, title, publication date, and year of publication.

This lesson also discusses plagiarism. Plagiarism is easy to avoid if you just follow a few specific guidelines. Always credit a source, even if you write a paraphrase or summary. Otherwise, you are stealing from the creator of the ideas. And, when you are revising your research paper, you should always check carefully for plagiarism.

The framework of an argumentative research project provides the reader with your own opinion and commentary on the subject, integrated with that of your sources. When you revise your project, pay particular attention to the framework. Above all, a clear, concise argument will assist your reader in understanding your thesis and your research.

Inquiry is fatal to certainty.

—Will Durant

LESSON RESOURCES

Textbook: Mauk and Metz: *Inventing Arguments*
- Chapter 13, "The Research Guide: Documenting Sources," pp. 411–451
- Chapter 17, "Environment," pp. 514–527

Review:
- Chapter 5, "Hidden Layers," pp. 77–95

Video: "Documenting Research" from the series *The Writer's Odyssey*

LESSON GOAL

You will establish credibility as a researcher and give readers access to your research by documenting sources in a formal research paper.

LESSON LEARNING OBJECTIVES

1. Follow guidelines for avoiding plagiarism.

2. Document the argumentative research paper using either MLA or APA format.

3. Revise the research paper paying attention to the framework of the writer's argument (commentary and opinion) and interspersed references to sources for support or counterargument.

LESSON FOCUS POINTS

1. Why should a writer document external sources in an argumentative research project?

2. What is MLA documentation style? What is in-text citation in MLA style? What is a Works Cited page in MLA style?

3. What is the MLA citation format for books? What is the format for articles?

4. What is the MLA citation format for articles in a newspaper? Articles in a journal paginated continuously? Articles reprinted in an anthology? Encyclopedia article?

5. What is the MLA citation format for government publications? Pamphlets? Personal interviews? Personal letters or memos? Published letters? Television programs? Films? Musical compositions? Sound recordings? Lecture or speech? Advertisements? Works of art (painting, sculpture, photograph)? Performance?

6. What is the MLA citation format for electronic sources? Online books? Articles in online journals? Print articles from online databases? Abstracts? Websites? E-mails? Online/listserver postings? CD-ROMs? Online encyclopedias?

7. What is APA documentation style? What is in-text citation in APA style? How are references documented in APA style?

8. What is the APA citation format for books? Articles? Articles in magazines? Articles in newspapers? Articles in journals paginated continuously? Articles or chapters in an edited book? Encyclopedia articles?

---

9. What is the APA citation format for brochures? Personal interviews or letters? Television programs? Government publications?

10. What is the APA citation format for electronic sources? Articles in online journals? Journal article retrieved from a database? Website?

WRITERS INTERVIEWED

Robert Rivard, Editor, *San Antonio Express-News*, San Antonio, TX

Hampton Sides, Author, Santa Fe, NM

SUGGESTED WRITING ASSIGNMENTS

Consult with your instructor and the course syllabus about requirements for any of the assignments listed below.

1. Write an argumentative research paper or project framing your argument with commentary and opinion with in-text documentation and Works Cited.

2. Revise a paper you have written and develop it into a research document that includes a variety of sources. Use in-text documentation and list your sources.

> *What is research but a blind date with knowledge?*
> —Will Harvey

ENRICHMENT ACTIVITIES

Complete the following activities. An answer key and/or guidelines appear at the end of this lesson for each activity.

I. Writing Activity: In-text Documentation
Two excerpts from professional essays appear below.

For each brief passage below, integrate some of the information using a direct quote, paraphrase, or summary as if you were placing it into the body of a paper. Then provide an in-text citation using MLA format for each passage.

A. "Wildcatting for Water" by Karen Breslau (reprinted in *Inventing Arguments*, First edition, p. 428)

Lesson 8—Documenting Research

65

The American West was settled like this--by brash men jabbing at maps, decreeing where dams should go so lush cities and farms could rise from the desert. They succeeded in making water so cheap, so plentiful, and so ordinary that most Americans take it for granted. Now there's a new reality. A mix of drought, rampant growth, and increasingly tough environmental restrictions has left virtually every community in America facing a water shortage. Nearly half of the United States is now affected by drought. From the Chattahoochee to the Rio Grande to the Colorado, major rivers are running at record low flows-- leaving cities and farmers desperate for new sources of fresh water. "We are rapidly reaching the limits of our ability to build new infrastructure and redistribute water," says Peter Gleick of the Pacific Institute, a California think tank.

_____

_____

_____

_____

_____

_____

_____

_____

_____

_____

_____

_____

_____

_____

_____

_____

_____

_____

_____

_____

B. "Fantastic Ideals," by Jennifer Worley (reprinted in *Inventing Arguments*, 3rd edition, pp. 474–476)

The ideal is getting thinner and thinner. Flawlessness is required. In a culture where obesity is on the rise and imperfection is everywhere, images of super-thin beauty are causing women to doubt their worth. Next to every image of the super-thin ideal model, there should be a sign that reads: "Caution. Do not try to achieve this body at home. It could be harmful to your health and may cause psychological damage."

_____

_____

_____

_____

_____

_____

_____

_____

_____

_____

_____

_____

_____

_____

_____

_____

_____

_____

_____

_____

(If required, submit your responses to your instructor for evaluation.)

II. Writing Activity: Works Cited and References

Select two external resources you are using for your research for this assignment. If required, submit your responses to your instructor for evaluation.

A. Cite complete information for both sources in a list of sources in MLA format following MLA Guidelines for works cited including author, title, date of publication, publisher, place, etc.

B. Write a references list including author, title, date of publication, publisher, place, etc. for both sources in APA format following APA Guidelines for references.

_____

_____

_____

_____

_____

_____

_____

_____

_____

_____

_____

_____

_____

_____

_____

_____

_____

_____

_____

_____

_____

_____

_____

Lesson 8—Documenting Research

III. Writing Activity: MLA Works Cited

Use the list of sources below to prepare a Works Cited list using Modern Language Association (MLA) documentation format. If required, submit your responses to your instructor for evaluation.

- A book by John Mauk and John Metz entitled <u>The Composition of Everyday Life</u>. This is the second edition, and it was published in Boston by Thomson Wadsworth. The publication date is 2006.

- An article by Ralph Nader entitled "Bank Mergers Skip Along, Right Past the Customers." The article originally appeared in the <u>New York Times</u> on Sunday, November 12, 1995.

- An online article entitled "New Year's Resolutions: Why Do We Make Them When We Usually Don't Keep Them?" The article was published February, 17, 2004, by Indiana University, Media Relations on the website: http://newsinfo.iu.edu/news/page/normal/1206.html.

- A book published by a corporate author, American Automobile Association (AAA). The title of the book is <u>Tour Book: New Jersey and Pennsylvania</u>. It was published for AAA by Heathrow in 2001.

- A film entitled <u>Monty Python's The Meaning of Life</u>. The film was directed by Terry Jones in 1983. It appeared on DVD in 2004 and was distributed by Celadine.

ANSWER KEY

Answer	Learning Objectives	Focus Points	References

I. Writing Activity: In-Text Documentation
..................LO 2 ....FP 1, 2 .... video segments 2, 3; textbook, pp. 413–414, 429–430
(Your instructor will advise you about evaluating this assignment.)

II. Writing Activity: Works Cited and References
..................LO 2 ....FP 1, 2, 7 .... video segments 3, 4; textbook, pp. 415–416, 431
(Your instructor will advise you about evaluating this assignment.)

III. Writing Activity: MLA Works Cited
..................LO 2 ....FP 1–6 .... video segments 3, 4; textbook, pp. 415–428
(Your instructor will advise you about evaluating this assignment.)

American Automobile Association. <u>Tour Book: New Jersey and Pennsylvania.</u>
    Heathrow: AAA, 2001.

Mauk, John and John Metz. <u>The Composition of Everyday Life.</u> 2nd ed. Boston:
    Thomson Wadsworth, 2006.

<u>Monty Python's The Meaning of Life.</u> Dir. Terry Jones, 1983. DVD. Celandine, 2004.

Nader, Ralph. "Bank Mergers Skip Along, Right Past the Customers." <u>New York Times.</u>
    12 Nov. 1995.

"New Year's Resolutions: Why Do We Make Them When We Usually Don't Keep
    Them?" Indiana University, Media Relations. 17 Feb. 2004.
    <u>http://newsinfo.iu.edu/news/page/normal/1206.html.</u>

Lesson 8—Documenting Research

Lesson 9

Arguing with Agility

The sounder your argument, the more satisfaction you get out of it.
—Edgar Watson Howe

THEME

You are constantly required to make judgments about your surroundings, yourself, and others. Beyond judgments in everyday life, you as a student often engage in more complex judgments about values and the value of policies, behaviors, laws, products, attitudes, and even people. In your college life as well as your professional, civic, and family life, you will often attempt to convince others to accept your judgments and act according to your thinking. In the everyday world and in your collegiate life, the most frequent argument is that of social value and social worth and the effects of an act or policy or behavior or event.

In this lesson, you will examine the qualities of something that others and maybe even you do not see, so you must argue about the hidden value of that something. You will do more than argue an opinion; you must use the argument to reveal an issue or seek out topics that others might ignore or not recognize. You will once again look below the surface of your topic and peel away the various layers as you learn more about the topic.

Argument should be polite as well as logical.
—Alphonse de Lamartine

LESSON RESOURCES

Textbook: Mauk and Metz: *Inventing Arguments*

- Chapter 9, "Arguing Value," pp. 207–239
- Chapter 19, "Consumption," pp. 548–573

Video: "Arguing with Agility" from the series *The Writer's Odyssey*

LESSON GOAL

You will apply the analytical techniques and processes necessary to develop an argument about the social value of a policy, behavior, event, text, or act.

Neither irony nor sarcasm is argument.
—Rufus Choate

LESSON LEARNING OBJECTIVES

1. Develop a thesis on the social value of a policy, behavior, event, text, or act to write an argument on value.

2. Explore the topic to find a new way of thinking or seeing by examining the opposite point of view for an argument on value.

3. Emphasize the use of evidence and appeals to support an argument on value.

4. Develop counterargument for an argument on value.

LESSON FOCUS POINTS

1. Where is a good starting place for finding a topic for an argument on value?

2. How does a writer find an argument that will reveal something about the topic? Whom or what will the topic harm? Whom or what benefits from the topic? What are the hidden effects of the topic?

3. How should a writer develop a thesis for an argument on value? What are thesis troublemakers?

4. How does a writer develop support for an argument on value? What are analogies? What are allusions?

5. What are appeals to logic in an argument on value? What are appeals to value?

6. What are counterarguments, concessions, and qualifiers in an argument of value?

7. What should a writer consider when deciding where to place a thesis, give details about a subject, and include counterargument?

8. Why are audience and voice essential in an argument of value? What is irony? What is satire?

9. What are concessions and qualifiers? What is subtext?

10. Why is revision necessary in an argument of value?

11. Why is it important to help others accept the main claim and act accordingly?

WRITERS INTERVIEWED

Andy Alford, Assistant Metro Editor, *Austin American-Statesman*, Austin, TX

Adam Pitluk, Author and Novelist, Dallas, TX

Bob Ray Sanders, Editorial Columnist, *Fort Worth Star-Telegram*, Fort Worth, TX

Mike Trimble, Editor and Columnist, *Denton Record-Chronicle*, Denton, TX

SUGGESTED WRITING ASSIGNMENTS

Consult with your instructor and the course syllabus about requirements for any of the assignments listed below.

1. Write an argument of value, based on the social value of a policy, behavior, event, or text.

2. Read the article "Intoxitwitching: The Energy Drink Buzz," by Simon Benlow in your text, pp. 556–558. Write a review of Benlow's article. In your review, state an overall evaluative claim about the argument of value in the article. Support your evaluation by citing his use of evidence, appeals, and counterargument in his article.

> *It is an excellent rule to be observed in all disputes, that men should give soft words and hard arguments; that they should not so much strive to vex as to convince each other.*
>
> —Bishop John Wilkins

ENRICHMENT ACTIVITIES

Complete the following activities. An answer key and/or guidelines appear at the end of this lesson for each activity.

I. Writing Activity: Irony

Irony is the use of language to suggest something opposite of what is actually said. Below are some examples of ironic statements from irony.com. "Social Satire for the Masses."™

In the spaces below each statement, explain why you think the quote is ironic. If required, submit your responses to your instructor for evaluation.

1. A recent ISPOS poll found the following: 78% of college business majors said that one of their goals in life was "to make a lot of money" or "to succeed in their careers." A separate poll among high-level executives asked the participants to name the one thing they most wish they could have. The most common answer – "youth."

(from "Lonely at the Top" 13 Nov 2006)

_____

_____

_____

_____

_____

_____

_____

_____

2. Ever had crayon envy when you were in elementary school?

(from "The Origins of Class Consciousness" 3 Nov 2006)

_____

_____

_____

_____

_____

_____

_____

_____

3. This October, the World Wide Web crossed the million website mark. But, as we all know, quantity and quality are very different things.

    (from "If the World Wide Web were a City…" 2 Nov 2006)

    _____

    _____

    _____

    _____

    _____

    _____

    _____

    _____

4. Approximately, 172,000 new books were published in the United States last year. Yet it is estimated that only about 90,000 authors submitted manuscripts in the same time frame. What do these statistics tell us?

    (from "Ghostwriters: The Hidden Saviors of the Publishing Industry" 18 Oct 2006)

    _____

    _____

    _____

    _____

    _____

    _____

    _____

    _____

II. Writing Activity: Counterargument

When you write counterargument, you address and refute an opposing position to your own argument. Writers often use counterargument as a tool for support in developing paragraphs. Some even use several paragraphs to set up an opposing position and counterargument. Others deliver counterargument in a separate paragraph immediately following the presentation of the opposing argument. The writers of the essays in your textbook all have various approaches to present counterargument.

Read the essay, "Letter to Kohl's" by K.T. Glency on pp. 548–553. Then write your response to the following questions on Glency's use of counterargument.

- What claims are made in defense of the topic?

- Why are those claims illogical, misguided, or unfair?

- What claims are made against the topic?

- Why are those claims illogical, misguided, or unfair?

In a brief essay, explain K.T. Glency's approach in presenting counterargument to Kohl's. Is Glency's approach effective?

If required, submit your responses to your instructor for evaluation.

_____

_____

_____

_____

_____

_____

_____

_____

_____

_____

_____

_____

_____

_____

_____

_____

III. **Writing Activity: Appeals to Logic and Value**
Examine the draft of your essay of value. Look at the ways you incorporated appeals to logic and value into your argument as you respond to the questions below.

Write responses to the following questions:
- To what situation, person, or thing does my topic relate?
- Have I appealed to any of these situations, persons, or things?
- What qualities do these situations, persons, or things share?
- How can I use those shared qualities to develop appeals to logic and value?
- What historical or current events or figures relate to my appeals?
- What literature reveals something about my appeals?
- What are the logical causes (direct and indirect) of the subject on a surrounding community or the broader society?
- What values does the subject compromise or challenge?

If required, submit your responses to your instructor for evaluation.

_____
_____
_____
_____
_____
_____
_____
_____
_____
_____
_____
_____
_____
_____
_____
_____
_____
_____
_____
_____
_____
_____

ANSWER KEY

Answer	Learning Objectives	Focus Points	References

I. Writing Activity : Irony
..................LO 2 ....FP 8 .... video segments 3, 4
(Your instructor will advise you about evaluating this assignment.)

II. Writing Activity: Counterargument
...............LO 2, 4 ....FP 6, 7 .... video segments 3, 4; textbook, pp. 548–553
(Your instructor will advise you about evaluating this assignment.)

II. Writing Activity: Appeals to Logic and Value
.................LO 3 ....FP 5 .... video segments 5, 6; textbook, pp. 232–233
(Your instructor will advise you about evaluating this assignment.)

Lesson 10

Arguing with Complexity

Close scrutiny will show that most 'crisis situations' are opportunities to either advance or stay where you are.

—Maxwell Maltz

THEME

Arguing with complexity is a difficult skill to master, particularly when writing about crisis. Dealing with crisis is a part of everyday life. The situations and questions arise, and the individual responds. In an argument of crisis, the most persuasive arguer is able to convince others what direction to follow. In this lesson, you will enhance your skills of argument to write with complexity about a crisis and its resolution. There are never only two sides in a crisis, so you must look beyond the obvious possibilities. When you react to a crisis, imagine the best possible options. Those options should be manageable, ethical, practical, economic, and far reaching. Try to see the hidden implications, blurred boundaries, and future consequences.

Sometimes arguments on crisis do not always need a solution. Often crisis arguments help the writer and the reader see the nature of a crisis rather than all the possible answers and outcomes. When you argue about crisis, you might employ the Hegelian dialectic or even accusation to define the crisis. But, hopefully, you will discover the myriad possibilities within any crisis.

When you face a crisis, you know who your true friends are.

—Earvin Magic Johnson

LESSON RESOURCES

Textbook: Mauk and Metz: *Inventing Arguments*
  • Chapter 10, "Arguing Crisis," pp. 241–281

Review: • Chapter 6, "Analyzing Argument," pp. 97–125
  • Chapter 17, "Environment," pp. 514–527

Video: "Arguing with Complexity" from the series *The Writer's Odyssey*

LESSON GOAL

You will respond to particular and real social crises with an argument about possible solutions.

LESSON LEARNING OBJECTIVES

1. Explore the various possibilities of action and potential solutions to an argument on a crisis.

2. Apply the Hegelian model to analyze the argument on crisis.

3. Logically arrange the argument with detailed support.

4. Use a variety of strategies to argue for the best possible options to resolve the crisis.

LESSON FOCUS POINTS

1. How does a writer determine the definition of a crisis?

2. What makes a situation a crisis and how is it a critical turning point? What are the possible outcomes? What could happen if nothing is done or if people make the wrong decisions?

3. Who or what caused the crisis? How did the crisis evolve? How long has the crisis existed? When might it end? Who or what will be affected by the crisis? What can be done to resolve it?

4. Why is it effective to conduct secondary research when writing an argument about crisis?

5. What are ways to develop a narrow thesis about crisis?

6. What is the Hegelian model? In the Hegelian model, what is thesis? Antithesis? Synthesis?

7. How will allusions help a writer develop an argument of crisis? Analogies? Authorities? Testimony?

8. How do appeals to logic and value help a writer develop an argument of crisis?

9. How can counterarguments, concessions, and qualifiers be valuable in developing an argument of crisis?

10. Where does a writer distinguish between the crisis and its solutions?

11. What are the chunks of an argument of crisis? How should a writer begin and conclude?

12. What is wonder and how does it aid a writer of an argument of crisis? Informality? Formality? Accusation?

13. Why should a writer of a crisis argument do a thorough revision in the areas of analysis, thesis, support, counterarguments, concessions, qualifiers, arrangement, audience, and voice?

WRITERS INTERVIEWED

Adam Pitluk, Author and Novelist, Dallas, TX

Gretchen Sween, Attorney and Writer, Susman Godfrey, LLP, Dallas, TX

Mike Trimble, Editor and Columnist, *The Denton Record Chronicle,* Denton, TX

SUGGESTED WRITING ASSIGNMENTS

Consult with your instructor and the course syllabus about requirements for any of the assignments listed below.

1. Write an essay about a particular crisis and develop an argument about possible action.

2. Read "Big House in the Wilderness: Moratoriums on Building and Individual responsibility," by Tracy Webster on pp. 250–252 and "Chief Seattle's Speech on the Land," on pp. 107–109 in your textbook. Both arguments provide different views on the topic of our environment. Select one of the essays and chart its argument. First, decide on the nature of each paragraph (description of the crisis, counterargument, etc.) Next, plot out its arrangement. Then, answer the following questions:

    *   What is the impact of the arrangement on the reader?

    *   How could the arrangement change to make the argument more intense or effective?

    *   At what points could the argument be more developed (using more detail)?

There cannot be a crisis today; my schedule is already full.

—Henry Kissinger

Lesson 10—Arguing with Complexity

81

ENRICHMENT ACTIVITIES

Complete the following activities. An answer key and/or guidelines appear at the end of this lesson for each activity.

I. Writing Activity: Hegelian Logic (dialectical reasoning)

Philosopher Georg Wilhelm Friedrich Hegel believed that all human thought developed through stages: personal to social to spiritual. A line of reasoning, as shown below, determined progression through the stages:

- Thesis (putting forward an idea)

- Antithesis (inevitable doubt of an idea)

- Synthesis (new understanding of an idea)

In this exercise, complete the antithesis and synthesis for each thesis below in the space provided. If required, submit your responses to your instructor for evaluation.

1. Thesis: Prime time television shows are ruining people's ability to think clearly.

   Antithesis: _____

   _____

   _____

   _____

   Synthesis: _____

   _____

   _____

   _____

2. Thesis: Many people vote against their own best interests.

   Antithesis: _____

   _____

   _____

   Synthesis: _____

   _____

   _____

   _____

3. Thesis: The government is not addressing our most basic human needs.

   Antithesis: _____

   _____

   _____

   _____

   Synthesis: _____

   _____

   _____

   _____

4. Thesis: To address tensions between the public and the police department, city government should develop a civilian review board for cases of officer misconduct.

   Antithesis: _____

   _____

   _____

   _____

   Synthesis: _____

   _____

   _____

   _____

II. Writing Activity: Accusation

Accusation is an effective tool because it takes a strong, stern stance. When you use accusation as a tool, you must be careful to not assume a caustic voice in your writing. Try to insert a paragraph of accusation into your own essay about crisis.

Paragraph of accusation:

_____

_____

_____

_____

_____

_____

_____

_____

Lesson 10—Arguing with Complexity

Respond in writing to the following questions about your own essay. If required submit your response to your instructor for evaluation.

1. Does the argument draw too much attention to my feelings?

_____

_____

_____

_____

_____

_____

_____

_____

_____

_____

_____

2. Is there someone to blame for the crisis? If so, can I accuse them without sounding too harsh?

_____

_____

_____

_____

_____

_____

_____

_____

_____

_____

_____

_____

Lesson 10—Arguing with Complexity

III. Writing Activity: Arrangement

Look at the outline of basic chunks of an essay on crisis on pp. 276–277 in your textbook. Try rearranging your draft for the argument of crisis in the space below. Include comments explaining why you moved chunks from one place to another. Label each chunk as it was in the beginning and as it is now. Is the result better than the original in your makeover? If required, submit your revision and comments to your instructor for evaluation.

_____

_____

_____

_____

_____

_____

_____

_____

_____

_____

_____

_____

_____

_____

_____

_____

_____

_____

_____

_____

_____

_____

_____

_____

ANSWER KEY

Answer	Learning Objectives	Focus Points	References

I. Writing Activity: Hegelian Logic
................LO 2 ....FP 6.. video segments 1, 2; textbook, pp. 270–271
(Your instructor will advise you about evaluating this assignment.)

II. Writing Activity: Accusation
................LO 4 ....FP 12 ....video segment 3; textbook, p. 279
(Your instructor will advise you about evaluating this assignment.)

III. Writing Activity: Arrangement
................LO 3 ....FP 11, 13 .... video segments 5, 6; textbook, pp. 276–277
(Your instructor will advise you about evaluating this assignment.)

Lesson 11

Arguing with Intensity

Future: that period of time in which our affairs prosper, our friends are true, and our happiness is assured.

—Ambrose Bierce

THEME

What better way to argue with intensity than to argue about future possibilities? In this lesson, you will investigate the relationship between the past and the future on a theoretical basis. You will argue not for what you want to happen, but what will happen despite your individual wishes. This lesson will guide you through a specific analysis of your adventurous thinking about possible futures. You will construct valid arguments about the most likely or most probable future.

You see evidence of the possibilities of the future everywhere in everyday life. Horror and science fiction films warn you of impending, perilous futures. Advertisements tell you that your future will be one of conveniences with a vast array of products and services. Since the future is hypothetical, you must make a strong argument to create a version of the future based on the past and present. Think about what has happened, what is likely to happen, and what could possibly happen. In your argument, you must convince readers that your prediction of the future is the most reasonable and the most objective. Use the tools provided you in this lesson to write an argument of intensity about the future.

You are led through your lifetime by the inner learning creature, the playful spiritual being that is your real self. Don't turn away from possible futures before you're certain you don't have anything to learn from them.

—Richard Bach

LESSON RESOURCES

Textbook: Mauk and Metz: *Inventing Arguments*
- Chapter 12, "Arguing the Future," pp. 323–357
- Chapter 20, "Popular Culture and the Media," pp. 575–585

Video: "Arguing with Intensity" from the series *The Writer's Odyssey*

LESSON GOAL

You will communicate your vision of the future by connecting what has happened with what is happening and what is likely to happen.

LESSON LEARNING OBJECTIVES

1. Develop an argument using rhetorical strategies to convince readers that a vision of the future is likely or possible.

2. Arrange the argument to maintain audience empathy and focus.

3. Balance intensity with credibility to develop the writer's voice in building an argument about a particular topic in the future.

LESSON FOCUS POINTS

1. How does a writer invent a particular view of the future?

2. Where does a writer begin writing an argument about a particular topic in the future?

3. How does a writer narrow the thesis? How does a writer analyze the topic? How does the writer develop a thesis that reveals a new way of looking at the future?

4. How do allusions, analogies, statistics, and authorities assist a writer in developing an argument about the future?

5. How do appeals to logic and character help a writer?

6. How do present resources (novels, films, poems, history, behaviors, policies, animals, institutions, laws, etc.) assist a writer in developing appeals and evidence?

7. How might counterarguments, concessions, and qualifiers assist a writer arguing about the future?

8. What arrangement best captures the reader's interest in an argument about the future? How should a writer connect the present and future? What is the most intense way to begin?

9. How can a writer avoid the formula essay?

10. How can a writer create intensity and credibility?

11. How might a writer revise intense writing and ideas?

WRITERS INTERVIEWED

Andy Alford, Assistant Metro Editor, *Austin American Statesman,* Austin, TX

Ben Fong-Torres, Journalist, San Francisco, CA

Richard Rodriguez, Essayist and Journalist, San Francisco, CA

Hampton Sides, Author, Santa Fe, NM

Gretchen Sween, Attorney and Writer, Susman Godfrey, LLP, Dallas, TX

SUGGESTED WRITING ASSIGNMENTS

Consult with your instructor and the course syllabus about requirements for any of the assignments listed below.

1. Connect the present and past to the future in an argument on a particular topic about the future.

2. Read the essay by Jay Harrington on pp. 581–583 in your textbook entitled "The Origin of Grunge." Interview someone who plays or likes punk or grunge music. Develop interview questions that will get at why the person enjoys grunge. How does your personal interview support or refute Harrington's argument that grunge and punk represent "alternative culture"?

> *I look to the future because that's where I'm going to spend the rest of my life.*
>
> —George Burns

ENRICHMENT ACTIVITIES

Complete the following activities. An answer key and/or guidelines appear at the end of this lesson for each activity.

I. Writing Activity: Beginnings
When you are arguing with intensity about the future, you should pay particular attention to your first sentence. You are setting the tone, establishing your voice, creating expectation, and providing necessary background. You may want to begin with one of the following:

A. Question

B. Anecdote

C. Quote

Lesson 11—Arguing with Intensity

89

D. Definition

E. Allusion

F. Description

Identify each item in the numbered list below using the alphabetized list:

_____ 1. "The wiring of emotional experience and the coding of that experience into memory is much more tightly integrated in women than men," according to psychologist Turhan Canli.

_____ 2. Each was presented with pictures of mundane objects, such as bookcases and fireplugs, and of objects expected to evoke strong emotions, such as guns, gravestones, corpses, and electric chairs.

_____ 3. All the disciplines define *humans* in particular ways: as tool-using animals, as symbol users, as spiritually motivated beings, as conscious dreamers, etc.

_____ 4. Why, may I ask, are you dressed as if you are going to the Monsters' Ball?

_____ 5. The coffee shop is more than a location for doing homework. On any given day, several tables will be pushed together while a group of students work together on a project, their papers and notebooks scattered between coffee cups and half-eaten bagels.

_____ 6. Like mortally wounded tyrannosaurs, they thrash about in frenzy, seeking enemies, destroying thousands of innocent lives with each blind spasm of reaction. And still the city creeps closer.

Possible answers appear in the answer key at the end of the lesson.

II. **Writing Activity: Syllogistic Premises**
Syllogisms are helpful as evidence in appealing to logic in an argument about the future. A syllogism is a logical formula or line of reasoning in which the conclusion depends on two premises.

A. Review pp. 348–350 in your textbook before reading the excerpt below from Jada's draft of her essay. Then respond to the following questions:

1. What line of reasoning does Jada want her readers to accept?
2. What premises about the past, present, and future must Jada's readers accept?

Excerpt from Jada's Draft

Some athletes will use any substance to create a competitive advantage. Steroids were first developed in the 1960s for children with degenerative diseases like leukemia, to keep their weight and strength up. They quickly found their way into Olympic and professional sports as athletes looked for a competitive edge. Now, more sophisticated drugs like Human Growth Hormone, or HGH, are being used by athletes to boost muscle mass and aerobic performance. As scientists are now experimenting with genetic modification in an effort to cure diseases and restore tissue, and as genetic modification offers endless possibilities for altering your body, it is inevitable that athletes will use genetic modification to further improve performance.

_____

_____

_____

_____

_____

_____

_____

_____

_____

_____

_____

_____

_____

_____

_____

_____

_____

_____

_____

_____

_____

Lesson 11—Arguing with Intensity

B. Review your own draft of your argument about the future. Then, respond to the following questions:

1. What line of reasoning do you want your readers to accept?
2. What premises about the past, present, and future must your readers accept?

_____

_____

_____

_____

_____

_____

_____

_____

_____

_____

_____

_____

_____

_____

_____

_____

_____

_____

_____

_____

If required, submit your responses to your instructor for evaluation.

III. Writing Activity: Urgency and Credibility

If you wish to have a clear voice in your writing, several techniques are available. When you write your argument about the future, try urgency and credibility to intensify your writing as described on pp. 354–355 in your textbook. For practice, rewrite the passage from Jada's draft of her essay below. Include urgency, credibility, and strong active verbs in your revision. If required, submit your response to your instructor for evaluation.

"The New Farm Team"

Imagine a young couple. Like many young couples, they want to have a baby—but not just any baby. This couple is determined to have a sports star, the next Tiger Woods or Lance Armstrong. So they consult a doctor—but not just any doctor. They see a specialist in genetic modification, who will arrange the baby's genes to predetermine extraordinary ability and endurance. Together, they will grow the perfect athlete.

_____
_____
_____
_____
_____
_____
_____
_____
_____
_____
_____
_____
_____
_____
_____
_____
_____
_____

Lesson 11—Arguing with Intensity

93

ANSWER KEY

	Learning	Focus	
Answer	Objectives	Points	References

I. Writing Activity: Beginnings
1. C .... LO 1, 2 .... FP 2, 4 .... video segments 1, 3, 4; textbook, pp. 346–350
2. B .... LO 1, 2 .... FP 2, 4 .... video segments 1, 3, 4; textbook, pp. 346–350
3. D .... LO 1, 2 .... FP 2, 4 .... video segments 1, 3, 4; textbook, pp. 346–350
4. A .... LO 1, 2 .... FP 2, 4 .... video segments 1, 3, 4; textbook, pp. 346–350
5. F .... LO 1, 2 .... FP 2, 4 .... video segments 1, 3, 4; textbook, pp. 346–350
6. E .... LO 1, 2 .... FP 2, 4 .... video segments 1, 3, 4; textbook, pp. 346–350

II. Writing Activity: Syllogistic Premises
.... LO 1 .... FP 3, 10 .... video segments 1, 2; textbook, pp. 348–350
(Your instructor will advise you about evaluating this assignment.)

III. Writing Activity: Urgency and Credibility
.... LO 1, 3 .... FP 8, 10, 11 .... video segment 5; textbook, pp. 354–355
(Your instructor will advise you about evaluating this assignment.)

Lesson 11—Arguing with Intensity

Lesson 12

Arguing Arguments

It is better to debate a question without settling it than to settle a question without debating it.

—Joseph Joubert

THEME

In this lesson, you will gather tools to evaluate the structure and hidden layers of the arguments of others and take a related position of your own. When coming into an argument, there is always space for you to create a side of your own. Arguments are not just two sided. In reality, arguments are multi-dimensional. You will make claims about the rhetoric of the argument you choose to evaluate, and you will make claims about the strategies of the arguers and the value of their perspectives.

Often, you might enter an argument that is already under way. If you do, use the sophisticated rhetorical tools in this lesson to shed light on the issues in the argument rather than shutting down the opponents. Good arguments often emerge from complexity from the arguers: acknowledging the details of the argument and acknowledging the arguments that came before. When you argue an argument, go beyond agreement or disagreement. Understand the argument you are addressing. Apply the tools of argument to take your own position.

Nothing is as frustrating as arguing with someone who knows what he's talking about.

—Sam Ewing

LESSON RESOURCES

Textbook: Mauk and Metz: *Inventing Arguments*
- Chapter 21, "Technology," pp. 587–600

Review:
- Chapter 6, "Analyzing Argument," pp. 97–125
- Chapter 8, "Arguing Causes," pp. 169–205

Video: "Arguing Arguments" from the series *The Writer's Odyssey*

Lesson 12—Arguing Arguments

95

LESSON GOAL

You will communicate a position on a public argument using rhetorical tools to reveal important values and unstated assumptions.

LESSON LEARNING OBJECTIVES

1. Develop a thesis that states a position on an external argument.

2. Make claims about the original argument, the strategies of the arguer, and the values of the perspectives involved.

3. Analyze the values and assumptions of the audience in developing support for the argument.

4. Revise the argument with assistance from peers.

LESSON FOCUS POINTS

1. How does a writer argue an argument? Does the writer choose a side? Or can a writer explore a variety of positions?

2. How does a writer select a written argument to argue about?

3. How do you analyze an argument? What should you consider when examining the argument of someone else?

4. How do you bring new ideas to arguing an argument? How is secondary research helpful? What are ways to develop the thesis when arguing an argument?

5. What is a "third path"? What are the broader categories for claims?

6. How do you develop support for arguing an argument? How is summary helpful? What about allusions? What about authorities?

7. What about appeals to logic? Value? Appeals and counterarguments? How are they helpful in arguing an argument?

8. When should you quote the original argument? When should you summarize? How much detail is necessary from the original argument or debate?

Lesson 12—Arguing Arguments

9. What should you know about audience and voice in arguing an argument? What about satire? How is it useful in arguing an argument?

10. What about revision? What should you consider doing if your thinking has changed in arguing the argument?

11. Why is it helpful for the writer to invent revision questions in arguing an argument?

WRITERS INTERVIEWED

Richard Rodriguez, Essayist and Journalist, San Francisco, CA

Gretchen Sween, Attorney and Writer, Susman Godfrey, LLP, Dallas, TX

Bob Ray Sanders, Editorial Columnist, *Fort Worth Star-Telegram*, Fort Worth, TX

Hampton Sides, Author, Santa Fe, NM

Ben Fong-Torres, Journalist, San Francisco, CA

Mike Trimble, Editor and Columnist, *Denton Record-Chronicle*, Denton, TX

SUGGESTED WRITING ASSIGNMENTS

Consult with your instructor and the course syllabus about requirements for any of the assignments listed below.

1. State your position on an external argument in an essay about arguing an argument. Make claims about the rhetoric of the argument, the strategies of the arguers, and the value of the perspectives involved.

2. Read the essay by Ross Wheatley on pp. 588–591 in your textbook entitled, "The Technology Slaves." Discuss the issue of slavery to technology with several classmates and technology specialists. Analyze the values and assumptions they bring to the discussion. Summarize your findings in a brief essay including your own position on technological slaves.

> *Where there is much desire to learn, there of necessity will be much arguing, much writing, many opinions; for opinions in good men is but knowledge in the making.*
>
> —John Milton

ENRICHMENT ACTIVITIES

Complete the following activities. An answer key and/or guidelines appear at the end of this lesson for each activity.

I. Writing Activity: Analyzing an Argument
Watch Rosa's argument in the video for this lesson ("Arguing Arguments").
Respond to the questions about her argument in the spaces below.

- What argument is Rosa responding to?

- What values are important to Rosa, and what role do they play in her argument?

- What role does the complex underlying issue of "lifestyle" play in Rosa's argument?

If required, submit your responses to your instructor for evaluation.

_____
_____
_____
_____
_____
_____
_____
_____
_____
_____
_____
_____
_____
_____
_____
_____
_____
_____
_____

II. Writing Activity: Organizing an Argument about Arguments

As you develop your argument, keep in mind the rhetorical strategies you will use. First, pay attention to your thesis about an ongoing argument. How will you find a place within the various positions in the original argument? Review pp. 191–194 in the textbook, and think about how you will focus your own thesis. Write a thesis below for your argument using one of the bulleted approaches in the textbook.

Original argument: _____

Approach: _____

Thesis: _____

When you determine the evidence to support your thesis about an existing argument, what strategies will you use? Will you use summary, allusions, authorities, appeals to logic or value, or appeals and counterarguments? (See pp. 195–197) In the space below, identify one strategy and write a brief passage based on your thesis that would support your argument.

Strategy: _____

Passage based on thesis:

_____
_____
_____
_____
_____
_____
_____
_____
_____
_____
_____
_____
_____
_____
_____
_____
_____

Arrangement is very important to writing an argument. How will you arrange your argument based on your thesis and the strategies you intend to use? Review pp. 198–200 in the textbook and respond in the space below to the questions about the arrangement of your argument.

- When will I quote the original argument?
- Where will I summarize the original argument or debate?
- How much detail will I include from the original argument or debate?

If required, submit your responses to your instructor for evaluation.

_____

_____

_____

_____

_____

_____

_____

_____

_____

_____

_____

_____

_____

_____

_____

_____

_____

_____

_____

_____

Lesson 12—Arguing Arguments

III. Writing Activity: Revision

Review your own argument about an argument. For revision purposes, answer the following questions:

- What questions do you ask yourself when you revise your work?
- How has your thinking changed since you first began examining the argument?
- How can you focus or improve your thesis?
- What types of support in the argument are most helpful?
- What opinions and details could you explore further to strengthen your argument?
- Does your argument anticipate the reader's response and counterargue effectively?
- What points have you conceded or qualified?
- How is your argument connected to other arguments?
- How might your ideas be better arranged to give your argument more momentum?

If required, submit your responses to your instructor for evaluation.

_____
_____
_____
_____
_____
_____
_____
_____
_____
_____
_____
_____
_____
_____
_____
_____
_____
_____
_____
_____
_____

ANSWER KEY

Answer	Learning Objectives	Focus Points	References

I. Writing Activity: Analyzing an Argument
...............LO 2, 3 ....FP 3, 5 .... video segments 1–4; textbook, pp. 188–190
(Your instructor will advise you about evaluating this assignment.)

II. Writing Activity: Organizing an Argument about Arguments
.............LO 1, 2, 3 ....FP 1–9 ....video segment 1; textbook, pp. 191–200
(Your instructor will advise you about evaluating this assignment.)

III. Writing Activity: Revision
.................LO 4 ....FP 10, 11 .... video segments 5, 6; textbook, pp. 204–205
(Your instructor will advise you about evaluating this assignment.)

Lesson 12—Arguing Arguments
102
© 2013 Cengage Learning. All Rights Reserved. May not be scanned, copied or duplicated, or posted to a publicly accessible website, in whole or in part.

Lesson 13

Finding Hidden Arguments

Somewhere, something incredible is waiting to be known.
—Carl Sagan

THEME

This lesson focuses on the disguises used to hide arguments and particular strategies for seeing through them. Arguments often wear the disguises of simple statements, reports, and inspiring messages. Arguments are also hidden in advertisements, songs, images, cartoons, bumper stickers, television shows, films, literature, and photographs. Your purpose in this lesson is to reveal an argument that people would otherwise not recognize.

In a hidden argument, regardless of the writer's intent, the text can deceive readers, send them mixed signals, or even prompt them to believe something contrary to its core message. Various strategies can serve as disguises to hide an argument:

- Objectivity fools the audience into thinking that the information is unbiased.
- Personal taste camouflages an argument in appeals to the personal tastes and desires of the audience.
- Spin is a set of rhetorical moves that change the meaning of an event or statement.
- Propaganda is a complex set of strategies used to drive readers toward a uniform way of thinking and feeling.

Hopefully, you will be able to see through these disguises when you encounter them in everyday life. As you present your argument about hidden meanings, think specifically about the techniques used in magazines, television, political ads, advertising, and bumper stickers to disguise subtle messages. Discuss disguises, so your argument clearly makes its point to your audience.

There is nothing like looking if you want to find something. You certainly usually find something if you look, but it is not always quite the something you were after.
—J. R. R. Tolkien

LESSON RESOURCES

Textbook: Mauk and Metz: *Inventing Arguments*
- Chapter 22, "Philosophy and Humanity," pp. 603–619

Student Course Guide: Diane Martin, *The Writer's Odyssey Student Course Guide*
- Appendix—Understanding Writer's Voice, pp. 111–118

Review:
- Chapter 5, "Hidden Layers," pp. 77–95
- Chapter 15, "Men and Women," pp. 471–492
- Chapter 20, "Popular Culture and the Media," pp. 575–585

Video: "Finding Hidden Arguments" from the series *The Writer's Odyssey*

LESSON GOAL

You will communicate the ability to recognize strategies used to disguise arguments and develop rhetorical strategies to present a position about a hidden argument.

LESSON LEARNING OBJECTIVES

1. Identify objectivity, personal taste, spin, and propaganda in a hidden argument.

2. Analyze text, context, subtext, and the target audience of the hidden argument.

3. Employ a writer's voice that invites the audience to examine the hidden argument.

LESSON FOCUS POINTS

1. What strategies help a writer locate a hidden argument and reveal its disguise?

2. How might you find hidden arguments in songs, slogans, advertisements, speeches, and greeting cards? How do you analyze a text to understand the subtle clues of hidden argument?

3. What should you know about text, context, and subtext to find a hidden argument?

4. What is a target audience, and what should you know about it in locating an argument in disguise?

Lesson 13—Finding Hidden Arguments

104

5. What techniques are helpful in developing and narrowing a thesis about hidden argument?

6. How can personal testimony and analogies assist in providing support?

7. How can appeals to logic and value assist in providing support?

8. How can counterarguments, concessions, and qualifiers assist in providing support?

9. Where should you summarize or explain the original text in a hidden argument? How should you include subtext and context?

10. What is the value of explicit versus implied thesis statements?

11. How do you create invitations in writing and how are they helpful? What is sentence variety, and how is it helpful?

12. Why should you consider the original argument in revising an essay about hidden argument? Has the original argument been represented fairly? How might representation of the original argument be fairer? Has the argument been treated with the respect it deserves?

WRITERS INTERVIEWED

Elizabeth Crook, Author and Novelist, Austin, TX

Adam Pitluk, Author and Novelist, Dallas, TX

James Ragland, Columnist, *The Dallas Morning News,* Dallas, TX

Bob Ray Sanders, Editorial Columnist, *Fort Worth Star-Telegram,* Fort Worth, TX

Hampton Sides, Author, Santa Fe, NM

Gretchen Sween, Attorney and Writer, Susman Godfrey, LLP, Dallas, TX

Ben Fong-Torres, Journalist, San Francisco, CA

Mike Trimble, Editor and Columnist, *Denton Record-Chronicle,* Denton, TX

Judy Yung, Historian and Author, Santa Cruz, CA

SUGGESTED WRITING ASSIGNMENTS

Consult with your instructor and the course syllabus about requirements for any of the assignments listed below.

1. Write an analysis of a hidden argument to reveal its disguise.

2. Read magazine articles to find a hidden argument about entrepreneurial greed, public rights, or finite resources (Refer to Chapter 20 in your text, "Ad Nation," by Wayne Grytting, pp. 584–585). Analyze the text and target audience of the hidden argument. Write an essay summarizing your opinion and your findings.

> *Maybe it's like this, Max. You know how, when you are working on a long and ordered piece, all sorts of bright and lovely ideas and images intrude. They have no place in what you are writing, and so if you are young, you write them in a notebook for future use. And you never use them because they are sparkling and alive like colored pebbles on a wave-washed shore. It's impossible not to fill your pockets with them. But when you get home, they are dry and colorless. I'd like to pin down a few while they are still wet.*
>
> —John Steinbeck

ENRICHMENT ACTIVITIES

Complete the following activities. An answer key and/or guidelines appear at the end of this lesson for each activity.

I. Writing Activity: Deconstruction
Read the essay, "Fantastic Ideals" by Jennifer Worley on pp. 474–477 in Chapter 15 of your text. Then review the following information about deconstruction.

> *Deconstruction* is a school of thought based on the idea that the inner workings of language can be revealed. Outside this highly theoretical tradition, people use the term deconstruction to mean "tear apart" or "break down." More precisely, "to deconstruct" means "to reveal how something works, to take down the outer coating so that the internal processes are shown." Once these processes are revealed, they lose their power. In the case of arguments, they lose their grip on consciousness. Deconstructing an emotional appeal, then, results in diffusing its power over audiences.
>
> (Mauk and Metz, *Inventing Arguments*, 1st edition)

Try to "deconstruct" Worley's argument by revealing the inner workings of her language. Try to take down the "outer coating" to show the inner processes. Write your own "deconstructed" version of Worley's essay. If required, submit your response to your instructor for evaluation.

_____

_____

_____

_____

_____

_____

_____

_____

_____

_____

_____

_____

_____

_____

_____

_____

_____

_____

_____

_____

_____

_____

_____

_____

_____

_____

Lesson 13—Finding Hidden Arguments

II. Writing Activity: Voice

Review the excerpts from the drafts below by Jada, Rosa, and Mitch in the lesson video. Analyze the three writers' use of voice. Do they extend an invitation to the reader? Do they vary their sentences to help the writing flow? What suggestions would you give each writer to assist in improving voice? If required, submit your responses to your instructor for evaluation.

Excerpt from Jada's Draft

The term "shock and awe" was initially used to spin the war by focusing attention on military pyrotechnics and away from its consequences. But as the term gathered momentum, it functioned more and more as propaganda. Critical thought and dissent were drowned out by a saturation bombing of our collective consciousness—we were the ones who were shocked and awed into submission by the power of our own propaganda.

Ironically, "shock and awe" didn't bomb the enemy into total submission. Instead, it ignited the anger that would develop into a mounting insurgency. It didn't work on the enemy, but it worked on the American people. It took a couple of years before they recovered their senses and began to fight back against the propaganda that had paralyzed them.

Analysis and revision:

_____

_____

_____

_____

_____

_____

_____

_____

_____

_____

_____

_____

Lesson 13—Finding Hidden Arguments

108

Excerpt from Rosa's Draft

The other context, though, is the Internet, or cyberspace. Because "The Cloud Appreciation Society" is a website, a virtual space, it's one only dedicated surfers are going to find. So, they're using the Internet to reach people who spend too much time on their computers, in order to encourage them to get away from their computers! Then, ironically, they spend more time looking at the clouds on their computers. The two contexts contradict each other, it seems. But who cares, if it gets you to notice the clouds!

The Cloud Appreciation Society isn't just promoting clouds. It's promoting the idea that clouds can set you free. As their ad states, "They are for dreamers and the contemplation of them benefits the soul. Indeed, all who consider the shapes they see in clouds will save on psychoanalysis bills." Clouds are free therapy. And you don't need an appointment.

Analysis and revision:

_____

_____

_____

_____

_____

_____

_____

_____

_____

_____

_____

_____

_____

_____

_____

_____

_____

_____

Excerpt from Mitch's Draft

You've got to hand it to the advertising executives; they really nailed it. Most men can't resist this image of themselves as some kind of endangered species of American masculinity. Am I right, cowpoke? Aren't you lonesome for a better way of life? Would a pickup truck fix you right up?

Analysis and revision:

_____

_____

_____

_____

_____

_____

_____

_____

_____

_____

_____

_____

_____

_____

_____

_____

ANSWER KEY

	Learning Objectives	Focus Points		References

I. Writing Activity: Deconstruction
................LO 2 ....FP 1, 2, 12 .... video segments 3, 4; student course guide, p. 106, ...textbook, pp. 474–477
(Your instructor will advise you about evaluating this assignment.)

II. Writing Activity: Voice
................LO 3 ....FP 11 .... video segments 5, 6; textbook, pp. 164–165
(Your instructor will advise you about evaluating this assignment.)

Understanding Writer's Voice

From MAUK/METZ, *Inventing Arguments*, 2e. ©2009 Heinle/Arts & Sciences, a part of Cengage Learning, Inc. Reproduced by permission, www.cengage.com/permissions

Voice is the writerly identity created within a text. It is closely related to style (the personal or individualized use of language conventions, with attention to appropriateness, situation, and audience). It is easy to comment on the style of speakers: *Mike is deliberate. Sheila is an excitable speaker.* We simply observe people as they speak, and we come to conclusions about their individualized use of language and gestures. But when we read something, we cannot comment on the actual writer, only on the identity in the text: *Clark is very formal here. Tamera seems curious.* This identity is referred to as the voice of the writer, or the presence and character of the writer as it appears in the text.

All texts have a voice, even if it is formal, barely noticeable, formulaic, or monotonous. Some writers create a strong voice, one that comes out of the text boldly, while others keep their voices understated.

Formality/Informality

Formality is the adherence of a text to conventions of style and format. Writing that stays within conventions, that does not draw attention to itself by digressing or breaking with convention, is considered formal. While many other features dictate the degree of formality, the following are important factors:

Formal Writing
- Adheres to conventions of grammar and sentence structure
- Does not draw attention to itself with novel phrasing or dramatic shifts in tone
- Does not use much figurative language (metaphors or similes)
- Attempts to remain transparent—draws attention to ideas rather than to the sentences, words, and phrases themselves

Informal Writing
- Veers away from standard conventions
- Intentionally breaks rules of conventional grammar or sentence structure
- Draws attention to itself with unique or quirky phrasing
- Freely uses slang or street phrasing
- Draws attention to the writer (I, me), the reader (you), or both (we)

Of course, writing is not simply either formal or informal. It can range from very formal to very informal, with many possibilities between the two extremes.

Activities

1. Look at previous examples of your own writing, and describe its level of formality. Refer to specific words and sentences to support your description. How was the level of formality appropriate or inappropriate?

2. As a class, discuss the following: How formal should college writing be? What features distinguish college writing from other situations?

Voice and Word Choice

Word choice, perhaps more than any other aspect of writing, impacts the nature of voice. In "Consumed by the Other: What Spam Means," Judy Chu's word choice influences how we experience the ideas and the writer:

> While Spam's cyber-significance is a worthy subject in itself, I am drawn to a more fundamental and slippery question about the original meat product: Just what does it mean to eat Spam? Evoking visceral responses among consumers and citizens worldwide, Spam rivals the iconic status of Coca-Cola and McDonald's, which is not so surprising given its place in America's history of twentieth-century modernization and globalization. Having come of age during World War II, it is inextricably linked with our nation's ideals of democracy as well as its military presence abroad. While some, like a chef friend of mine, decry it as a nightmare of food technology, countless others, including most residents of our 50th state, relish its savory sweetness and rely upon its shelf life.

Chu's vocabulary creates the image of a reflective, formal, and careful thinker. And because the word choice is slightly more sophisticated than most everyday usage, Chu sounds more deliberate and perhaps more elegant than the person we may talk with at lunch or on the street. Imagine if Chu had selected more common words. Notice how the words change the reading experience—how we encounter Chu and how we are invited to think about the topic:

> While Spam's appearance on the Internet is interesting, I am curious about the original meat product and what it means. Around the world, people respond physically to Spam. It competes with big-name products like Coca-Cola or McDonald's, which is not surprising given Spam's place in America's technological and political growth.

As with all elements of writing, word choice depends on the situation: the topic, the readers, the writer, the rules and policies at hand, the time and place. Good writers always consider their readers; they try not to overwhelm them with vocabulary or (even worse) to perform feats of great thesaurus application. But good writers also help readers conjure new ideas. Good writers try to promote a fresh way of thinking, and fresh words are often a powerful tool to that end.

Voice and Sentence Variety

When sentence length does not vary, the writer's voice seems monotonous, dry, and lifeless. So good writers attempt to vary sentence length—developing longer sentences that bring readers into the complexities of an idea as well as shorter sentences to emphasize a specific point. In the following passage from Wendy Kaminer's article "Gender Bender," the variation of long and short sentences keeps the writer's voice from falling into a formulaic, monotonous pattern:

> I'm no expert on magnetic resonance imaging, but I've read that it's open to interpretation. And somehow I find these red blobs unconvincing as evidence that women are more emotionally retentive than men. You don't have to be a scientist to wonder whether a study suggesting that the emotional memories of 12 women were up to 15 percent more accurate than the emotional memories of 12 men is proof that men and women think differently; you merely need a knowledge of history. Scientific studies "proving" that men are smarter or more analytical and less emotional than women, or that men and women use their brains differently, are periodically trumpeted and more quietly debunked. Consider the conviction of 19th-century scientists, who posited that men were smarter than women because their brains were heavier. In 1880, former U.S. Surgeon General William Hammond asserted that "the brain of a woman is inferior in at least 19 different ways to the brain of a man."
>
> How did he know? Scientists hadn't studied the brains of women, as one of my favorite feminists, Helen Hamilton Gardener, pointed out. They were preoccupied with weighing the brains of famous men.

Sentence structure can be used to emphasize points and to create an insistent or urgent voice. Repeating a clause or phrase pattern can, for instance, make a voice (and the argument) seem more urgent and intense. In the following passage from Amber Edmondson's essay "Citizens and Consumers," the recurring when clauses create a voice that is committed and insistent:

> This economic system is a fairly young experiment that seems to contradict our natural tendencies toward community. When citizens in a community become simply consumers in an economy, they forget how to operate as a cooperative and the benefits of doing so. When local restaurants bow out to more expensive, more upscale operations like Ruby Tuesday, "regulars" disappear and servers lose that bond with their customers and their connection to the community. When local farmers are forced out of work by corporate farms and chain stores that stock food from unknown origins, communities lose a source of local food and quickly forget that food comes from anywhere but the supermarket.

Voice and Pronouns

Pronouns are first, second, or third person. First person refers to the person speaking (*I*, *me*, *we*). Second person refers to the person being spoken to (*you*). Third person refers to the person or thing being spoken about (*he*, *she*, *it*). There is no definite rule against using first- or second-person pronouns, but since the focus of most academic and professional writing is on the subject matter, not the writer or the reader, it often avoids using first- and second-person pronouns.

First-person references (*I*, *me*, *mine*) draw the reader's attention to the writer, not the subject being discussed. In some situations, using first-person pronouns can be an effective rhetorical strategy. But it can indicate that a writer is focusing too much on him- or herself and not enough on the subject matter. When writing about an issue, instead of saying, "I like violent movies" or "I think video games are educational; I've played them all my life," academic writers focus their language more on the issue: "Violent movies have been a controversial issue . . ."

Appendix—Understanding Writer's Voice

113

"Children now spend more time playing video games than . . . ." This is not to say that first-person references are forbidden. Some academic and professional writing does use first-person pronouns and achieves an appropriate emphasis on the subject matter. The subject matter and writer may, in fact, be one and the same. For instance, when a writer uses a personal testimony in an argument, the first-person pronoun I is essential.

Good writers are aware that any use of the first person automatically draws attention to the writer, not the subject. Consider these examples:

- I began by thinking out loud how it seems odd that men come here to hunt deer that you have to try not to hit with your car. (The writer draws attention to her own thinking.)
- It seems odd that men come here to hunt deer that motorists have to try not to hit with their cars. (Attention is focused more on the subject matter than on the writer's thoughts.)
- Hunters travel to Peace Valley to hunt deer so abundant they are a hazard to motorists. (The writer places herself in the background and her subject matter up front.)

Second-person pronouns (*you, your*) address the reader directly. They are seldom used in academic writing because the subject, not the reader, is at the center of attention. In informal or verbal exchanges, people often shift to "you" to refer to a generic person. Consider the following examples:

The airport is inadequate for our present needs. In the past ten years, the number of air travelers has tripled. You wait for over an hour at baggage claim, and then you have a hard time getting a cab. By this time, you are getting pretty angry.

The airport is inadequate for our present needs. In the past ten years, the number of air travelers has tripled. Passengers wait for over an hour at baggage claim, have a hard time getting a cab, and become frustrated with their flying experience.

The first example above unnecessarily involves the reader. The writer doesn't mean when *the reader* gets off the plane but means when *passengers in general* get off the plane. The pronoun reference, although understandable, is not accurate. Such unfocused references can draw the reader's attention away from the subject matter and even make inaccurate (and unintentional) statements about the reader. Consider the examples below, from a letter to a college newspaper:

The university should shovel and salt the sidewalks in the early morning before classes begin, not later that afternoon. You just about kill yourself, slipping and sliding to class through the snow. You're bound to be late for biology, which you're already failing

The writer could change her second-person pronouns to first-person, which is probably what she really means:

The university should shovel and salt the sidewalks in the early morning before classes begin, not later that afternoon. I just about kill myself, slipping and sliding to class through the snow. I'm bound to be late for biology, which I'm already failing.

By avoiding first and second person altogether, the writer could make the same point more effectively:

> The university should shovel and salt the sidewalks in the early morning before classes begin, not later that afternoon. Students and faculty could be seriously injured scurrying to class in such hazardous conditions.

Notice how in the examples above the writer has not just changed pronoun references, but, more importantly, has also revised her thinking. Her argument now reads as if she's concerned about the well-being of others, not only herself.

Voice and Asides

Any phrase, clause, or sentence that is slightly removed from the main focus is an aside. Asides briefly pull a reader's attention away from the primary flow of the sentence and offer a small comment (much like this statement in parentheses). Asides can be created with dashes, parentheses, or commas. They are sometimes used to clarify a point or qualify an argumentative claim. Notice Barcley Owens's quick clarification in parentheses:

> Hippocrates subscribed to Empedocles' notion of four fundamental elements and furthermore speculated that there were four specific properties: *cold, dry, wet,* and *hot.* He found that earth (composed of dirt, sand, rocks) was mostly cold and dry, whereas air was often hot and wet, and so forth.

Writers use asides to insert an intimate or personal expression or comment, which may lend informality and familiarity to their voice. Notice the informal voice and the asides in this argument about drug testing:

> Although I do not have statistics, if they even exist, I believe it is safe to say that the vast majority of D.U.I. arrests are alcohol-related. (Drug tests are not implemented to detect Coors and Budweiser.) The point here is that crack heads and "smackies" are not the ones we see pulled off to the side of the road doing the field sobriety tests. And they very rarely (if ever) manage to get jobs as airline pilots or airtraffic controllers.

Voice and Figurative Language

Figurative language refers to any words, phrases, or sentences that are not literal or that redirect meaning away from the literal definitions of words. It is used to help writers and speakers portray ideas and, if used appropriately, can add layers of richness to an argument. Figurative language often is categorized into the following common uses:

- **Analogy** is an extended comparison between two things that share characteristics or qualities, or between two situations or scenarios that are similar. An unfamiliar or less known thing usually is compared to something more familiar, thereby making the unfamiliar more familiar. Analogies can be used to bring out a particular quality:
  The U.S. military faced the same kind of consistent attacks in Iraq as the Russian military did in Afghanistan.

- **Antonomasia** replaces someone's actual name with a description, such as the *king of pop* to refer to Michael Jackson or the *godfather of soul* to refer to James Brown.

- **Hyperbole** is a deliberate exaggeration: *I've got a ton of homework.*

- **Irony** is the act (or art) of making a statement that is opposite of the intended meaning: *Nice job!* after someone trips over a shoelace.

- **Metaphor** is a comparison in which one thing takes on the characteristics of another: *This company is on the edge, and one wrong move could send it plunging downward.*

- **Metonymy** names something with only part of that thing, such as *Washington* to refer to the U.S. government or the *pen and the sword* to refer to writing and military action.

- **Personification** uses human qualities to describe a nonhuman thing: *The house just sat there through the years, minding its own business while the world went on around it.*

- **Simile** is a comparison using like or as in which one thing takes on the characteristics of another: *You are like a hurricane. There's calm in your eye* (Neil Young).

- **Understatement** is deliberately less forceful or dramatic than reality: *The Sahara desert is a little on the dry side.*

Figurative language is associated with informal writing, but it often is used in formal argument as well. In fact, some of the most formal arguments use figurative language. Notice this passage from the Declaration of Independence:

> Prudence, indeed, will dictate that Governments long established should not be changed for light and transient causes; and accordingly all experience hath shewn, that mankind are more disposed to suffer, while evils are sufferable, than to right themselves by abolishing the forms to which they are accustomed. But when a long train of abuses and usurpations, pursuing invariably the same Object evinces a design to reduce them under absolute Despotism, it is their right, it is their duty, to throw off such Government, and to provide new Guards for their future security.

Several phrases, such as the "long train of abuses" and "to throw off such Government," are subtle metaphors. While they do not draw attention to themselves as metaphors, they create important images. In fact, as this passage demonstrates, figurative language is so much a part of the English language that it often seems camouflaged, almost imperceptible to the eye. Notice the following subtle use by Ed Bell:

> But not just astronomers care about light pollution. And not just plants and animals are affected by it. Haas says that "two generations now live on our world never having seen our address in the Universe." He means the Milky Way, which gets erased each night by the washed-out skyglow that is caused by too much wasted lighting.

Wendy Kaminer uses figurative language more obviously:

> Women are hardwired to experience and recall emotions more readily than men, according to a study announced last month in the *Proceedings of the National Academy of Sciences,* as well as on CNN's morning show.

And so does Laura Tangley:

> These days, however, amid mounting evidence to the contrary, "the tide is turning radically and rapidly," says Marc Bekoff, a biologist at the University of Colorado-Boulder. Research by Bekoff and others— in fields ranging from ethology to neurobiology—is beginning to provide scientific support for the notion that animals feel a wide range of emotions. These findings, they believe, have profound implications for how humans and other species will interact in the future.

Activities

1. Make a list of figurative language that you use or hear in everyday life. Label each figure (metaphor, simile, etc.).

2. Write a paragraph about your day so far that overuses figurative language and overwhelms the reader.

Article titles can use figurative language:

> "Colleges Caught in a Vice," Stanley Fish
> "High-Tech Heroin," Richard Forno
> "A Pipe Dream: Real Reporting from Newsweek," Ben Stapleton

Sophisticated arguers can dispute figurative language. In other words, when an opponent uses a figure, some arguers will show why it is faulty. In Stanley Fish's New York Times article "Colleges Caught in a Vice," he critiques a familiar analogy:

> But this remedy [thinking about colleges like businesses] won't do anything except make the situation worse. If there is a crisis in college costs it has not been caused by price-gouging or bureaucratic incompetence on the part of universities; a better analogy would be the mass circulation magazines of the 1950s like *Collier's* and *Look,* which folded at the very point when they had more readers than ever. The problem was that production costs far outpaced the revenues from subscriptions and advertisers, and every new reader actually cost them money.

Likewise, Wayne Grytting, in his essay "Ad Nation," points to a problem with someone else's simile:

> In their search for emotionally compelling ideas, advertisers are running into a roadblock. It's getting harder and harder to reach consumers who are hit by an estimated 300 commercial TV messages a day. David Lubars, an ad executive with the Omnicom Group with an enviable literary touch, complained that consumers "are like roaches— you spray them and spray them and they get immune after a while." A truly humbling simile.

Grytting's simple final statement, "A truly humbling simile," quietly pokes fun at Lubars's questionable taste in comparing consumers to roaches.

Figurative language should be used with discretion. When overused, it can overwhelm an audience and obscure meaning. One sure way to confuse an audience is to mix metaphors: to use two or more metaphors with different meaning or images. For instance, notice the conflicting metaphors in following passages:

Appendix—Understanding Writer's Voice

117

The healthcare plan leaves both the small businesses and their employees out to dry. While the insurance companies continue making huge profits, business owners and everyday laborers are getting soaked with the bill.

This healthcare plan will protect our citizens and our future from the jaws of financial ruin. It will keep the health of the nation afloat for years to come.

The two metaphors in each passage compete with one another and keep the reader from settling on a clear image. While the language may sound grand, the message gets lost. Political arguments or ceremonial speeches can become overwhelmed by figurative language, blurring real messages with layers of metaphor

---

Activity

Make a list of clichés that you have heard or used. Explain the meaning behind them without using any of the terms in the clichés.

A Caution about Clichés

Clichés are worn-out expressions. They might get used in everyday situations (informal discussions, advertising, greeting cards, popular music, sitcoms, and talk shows), but they have little or no power in a sophisticated argument that attempts to develop ideas or change perspectives. Notice the following clichés:

> You don't know what you've got until it's gone.
> Live each day to the fullest.
> A mother knows best.
> People need to stand on their own two feet.
> People should pick themselves up by their bootstraps.
> Everyone is entitled to his or her own opinion.
> Walk the walk and talk the talk.

These phrases are conventional wisdom used in informal settings to support common ways of thinking. They do not make people think. They replace genuine thinking.

Some clichés are more noticeable than others. That is, we might recognize a phrase as worn-out more quickly than we notice others. Some phrases are so common that they can go almost undetected:

> With this plan in place, American workers can give it their all and make the country strong.

Here, give it their all is the cliché. It is used so often that the average reader may not even notice it. But the phrase is vague and actually interferes with the idea in the sentence. Because clichés can interfere with the development of ideas and substitute for inventive thinking, good writers avoid using them.